THE
WORLD
AT WAR
1914-1918

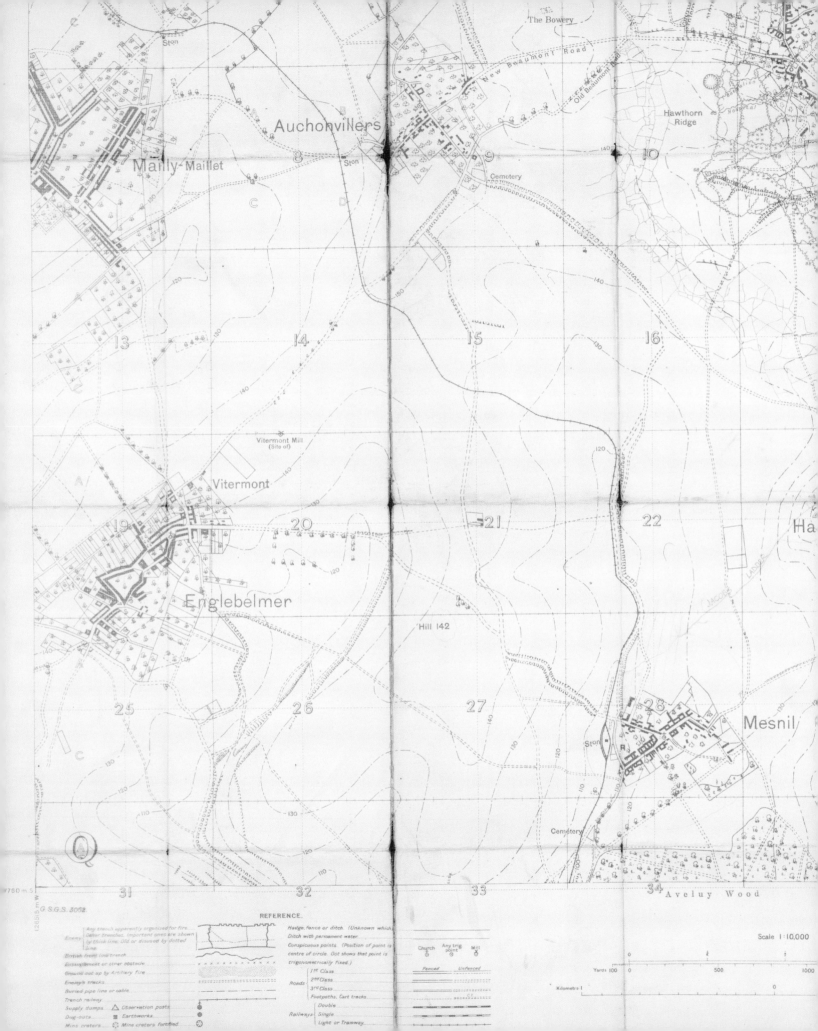

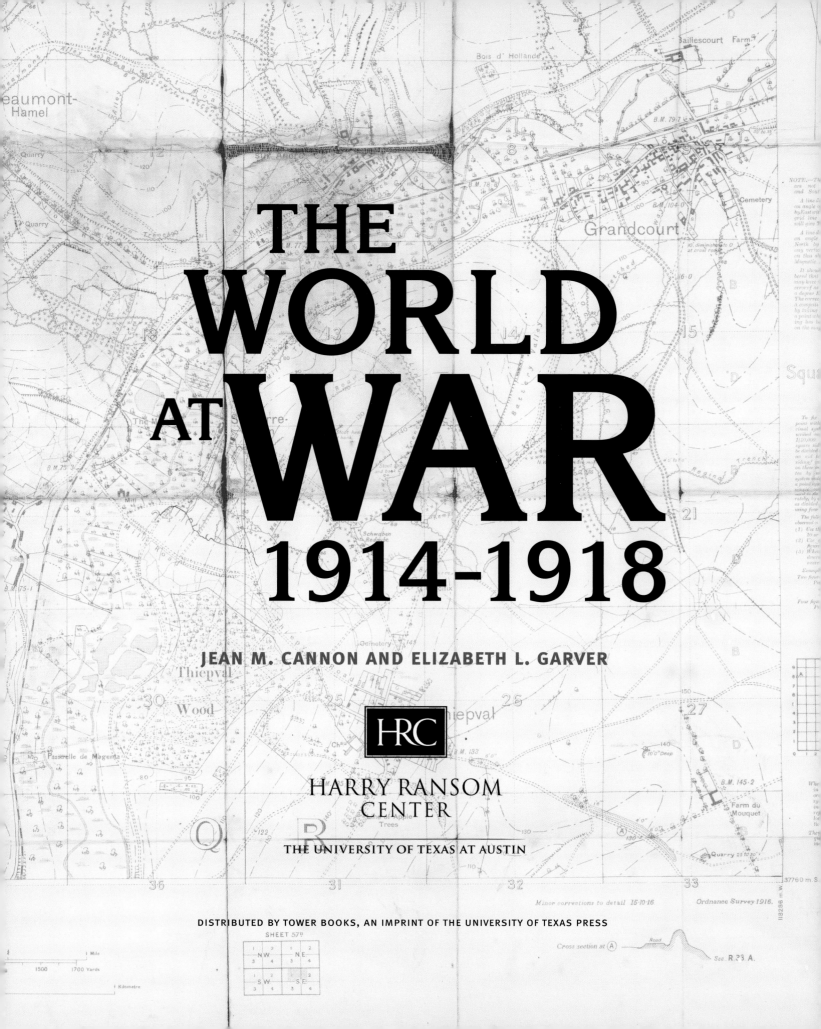

THE
WORLD
AT WAR
1914-1918

JEAN M. CANNON AND ELIZABETH L. GARVER

HRC

Harry Ransom
Center

THE UNIVERSITY OF TEXAS AT AUSTIN

DISTRIBUTED BY TOWER BOOKS, AN IMPRINT OF THE UNIVERSITY OF TEXAS PRESS

Library of Congress Control Number: 2013953347

ISBN 978-0-292-75754-7

TITLE, PAGES ii–iii
Detail of Blunden trench map

CONTENTS, PAGE vi
Disabled veterans returning home from
the Western Front (photograph)

FOREWORD, PAGE viii
Detail of German war dog (photograph)

INTRODUCTION, PAGE xii
Wounded soldiers awaiting transport
(photograph)

INDEX, PAGE 76
British pilots preparing for a raid into
enemy territory (photograph)

FRONT COVER
British infantry soldiers preparing
to attack German trenches
(photograph)

BACK COVER
"Back Him Up!" (poster)

The exhibition *The World at War, 1914–1918* and this companion publication were made possible through the generous support of the Cain Foundation.

Frank Denius is one of our most decorated soldiers of World War II. He fought with bravery and honor in the 30th Infantry Division in Europe and was involved in the D-Day invasion. Frank has remained a hero long after the hard-fought battles of the war came to an end. Through his generosity and leadership, he has made an incomparable impact on The University of Texas at Austin and the Harry Ransom Center. Frank has been involved in many of the Ransom Center's major initiatives, from our building renovation to the acquisition of several important cultural archives, from our research fellowship program to our centennial commemoration of World War I through this catalog and the complementary exhibition. The Ransom Center owes a great debt to Frank Denius, and we are proud to have such a fine and distinguished friend.

Additional thanks to Thomas F. Staley, Harry Huntt Ransom Chair in Liberal Arts, for his vision and leadership in making this exhibition possible.

Frank Denius, President of the Cain Foundation

CONTENTS

FOREWORD STEPHEN HARRIGAN

Tried hard not to die.

These wrenching words are from the careful notes Arthur Conan Doyle made after a séance in November 1918. They were uttered via a medium claiming to be in touch with Doyle's son Kingsley, who was wounded at the Somme and died of pneumonia a year later, in 1917. The inventor of Sherlock Holmes had a medical education but also a yearning, mystical mind, and in this remarkable document we see him wrestling with himself, needing to believe that he really is in contact with his dead son, skeptical enough to note where the medium's declarations and the facts diverge. "Calls me Dad," Doyle writes in the left-hand column of the page, where he records the words Kingsley is supposedly speaking through the medium; but on the right-hand side he offers a small, heartrending qualification: "That is good—usually Dadsy."

Arthur Conan Doyle's séance record, a raw glimpse into one father's grief, is one of the emotional cornerstones of this exhibition. But Kingsley Doyle was only one of the 37 million casualties of the Great War. From 1914 to 1918, grief engulfed the world. Since such global suffering, on such a staggering scale, is almost beyond the reach of human imagination, an exhibition like this one has its natural limits. The Ransom Center's exhibition *The World at War, 1914–1918* is not the story of the war itself; it's the story of the way the war touched the lives of both ordinary and legendarily exceptional people—how it left them inspired, degraded, ennobled, torn apart. The documents and artifacts assembled here give us a valuable firsthand picture of what it was like to be an individual, to be a family, to be a country helplessly swept up into a sudden, shattering storm.

It's easy to be stirred, even 100 years later, by the idealism and sense of sacred purpose that drove so many nations into the war and that kept driving them through it after the fighting on the Western Front degenerated into a static slaughter. The recruiting and propaganda posters are unnervingly bright and unfaded; they still carry a charge, and the national character traits they betray are still relevant. Here are the orderly British— workmen, barristers, gamekeepers—obediently queuing up beneath the headline "Step

>>> **Stephen Harrigan** is a longtime writer for *Texas Monthly,* and his articles and essays have appeared in a wide range of other publications as well, including the *Atlantic,* the *New York Times Magazine,* and *Slate.* He is the author of nine books of fiction and nonfiction, including the novels *The Gates of the Alamo* and *Remember Ben Clayton,* and serves as a faculty fellow at The University of Texas at Austin's James A. Michener Center for Writers.

into Your Place" to join the ranks of the fighting men marching off to the trenches. The French pitch to its citizenry is more passionate. "On les aura!" yells a solitary *poilu* (soldier) rendered in gray and brown charcoal. His arm is stretched theatrically outward as he looks back with a martyr's fervor toward the men he is leading into battle.

The United States did not come into the war until April of 1917, almost two and a half years after the conflict began, and the American posters on view in this exhibition depict a country still innocent of the war's modernist horrors, a country mobilized by a belligerent enough-is-enough attitude. America's task is clear: step in and put a stop to the mad German gorilla, the proto–King Kong that has been rampaging all over Europe.

There are also posters featuring galloping desert warriors in Algeria, along with stereoscopic photographs of British troops pursuing the Germans in East Africa, snapshots of Armenian refugees fleeing the Turks, a group portrait of the Russian women warriors who called themselves the "Battalion of Death," and an expensively bound limited first edition of T. E. Lawrence's *Seven Pillars of Wisdom*, his classic account of the guerrilla fighting in the Middle East. What these items in the exhibition demonstrate as vividly as any map is the fact that the phrase "World War" was not casually bestowed. The chaos that was unleashed by the assassination of Archduke Ferdinand in Sarajevo overlapped the earth, from Flanders Fields to the Suez Canal, from the coast of Chile to the Russian steppes.

Lawrence of Arabia is only one of the legendary World War I personages whose papers are housed in the Ransom Center and displayed for this exhibition. Edmund Blunden's trench maps and scouting notes, rendered so fastidiously and precisely, could be the work of an engineer rather than the influential poet he became. Here is a letter from Siegfried Sassoon to Ottoline Morrell, sent from Craiglockhart War Hospital, where the poet had been sent with a diagnosis of shell shock, when what he was really suffering from was an angry dissolution of belief in the purpose of the war and of the men in power who were waging it. We see 20-year-old William Faulkner, bored and restless and longing to reinvent himself, writing a letter to his parents from his Canadian Royal Air Force training camp in Toronto. He includes a drawing of the new uniform he covets but that, because of the Armistice, he will wear only in his dense imagination.

In a different key are two powerful letters from Wilfred Owen, another iconic poet of World War I. In one letter, to his 14-year-old brother, he has drawn a sketch of a man's head showing the entry and exit wounds caused by a bullet, and below it another sketch of a Zouave's leg with a ghastly hole in the calf. "I deliberately tell you all this to educate you to the actualities of war."

The actualities of war caught up with Owen a little over two years later, after he himself had been wounded by a trench mortar, left for dead, sent to Craiglockhart to recuperate along with Sassoon, and then returned to the front, where—according to his Military Cross citation—he "behaved most gallantly." The letter he wrote from a cellar in a French farmhouse a few weeks before the war's end are his last words to his mother. "It is a great life," he reassures her. "I hope you are as warm as I am; as serene in your room as I am here. . . . Of this I am certain you could not be visited by a band of friends half so fine as surround me here." He died a few days later in a raid across the Sambre-Oise Canal, but perhaps this shiningly happy letter gave his mother's anxious heart at least a temporary sense of peace.

Like most of the men who died in combat in the Great War, Wilfred Owen was killed by machine-gun fire. The creator of the machine gun is represented in the exhibition as well, in a photograph ablaze with cognitive dissonance. There is no date, but judging from the way the American inventor Hiram Maxim—whose previous gifts to the world included curling irons and mouse traps—sits behind the gun, sighting down the barrel with what looks like innocent exuberance, the picture was probably taken before mankind gained a full understanding of what Maxim's creation was capable of doing. Here he is in his bushy goatee and top hat, a self-made plutocrat, no doubt confident that his ingenious killing machine would help secure a brighter future for the world. But included in this exhibition are other images that Maxim could not have foreseen—a young corporal named Adolf Hitler, staring fiercely at the camera in a group photo with his comrades, perhaps already seething with poisonous insight gained at the front; a skeleton slowly collapsing into the putrescent earth, still wearing a helmet and gas mask, puttees still wrapped around one leg bone.

The memoirs, letters, posters, film clips, diaries, and tattered home-front scrapbooks assembled here all bear powerful witness to lives lost in the Great War, to exalted or notorious reputations created by it, to a world still trying to recover from it a hundred years later. We can inspect the contents of the display cases only through the distorting lens of history, which imposes a context and narrative logic that were never available to the people who left these objects behind. To them it was all new, all happening before their eyes. We can't perceive their world, and we can't summon them to ours, but like Arthur Conan Doyle we sense that they are still hovering just outside our field of awareness, dead but still burdened by what they had lived through, still bearing a message they want very much to deliver.

INTRODUCTION JEAN CANNON

The lamps are going out all over Europe. We shall not see them lit again in our time.
—Sir Edward Grey, 1914

The exhibition *The World at War, 1914–1918* (February 11–August 3, 2014) marks the centenary of the start of World War I. Triggered by the June 1914 assassination of Archduke Franz Ferdinand of Austria by a Bosnian-Serb student, open conflict began the following month when Austria-Hungary invaded the Kingdom of Serbia in retaliation. Within weeks, nearly all of the major nation-states of Europe were drawn into a war that lasted four long years and killed 10 million men. The trenches of the "war to end war" introduced the horrors of industrialized warfare in the form of the machine gun, tank, and poison gas. Meanwhile, home fronts faced threats of invasion and zeppelin attack, and whole societies were transformed by mass mobilization and an appalling global death toll. The collective personal and national trauma inflicted on all who experienced the war remains a potent touchstone that speaks to a contemporary world still embroiled in conflict.

Drawing on the Ransom Center's extensive cultural collections, this exhibition illuminates the lived experience of the war from the point of view of its participants and observers, preserved for a twenty-first-century generation through letters and diaries, memoirs and novels, photographs and drawings by battlefield artists, and propaganda posters and films. The visitor to *The World at War, 1914–1918* will better understand the monolithic history of the war through the archives of men and women who witnessed watershed events that ushered in the modern world as we know it. The exhibition also explores the long legacy of the conflict—one that still affects politics, culture, and human memory. Soldier-poet Wilfred Owen referred to those killed in battle as "our undying dead"; his friend the poet Siegfried Sassoon called them "the nameless names"; writer Gertrude Stein famously pronounced both the casualties and the survivors of the war the "Lost Generation." This exhibition seeks to recover the personal experience of the war and to pay homage to an event that changed forever human beings' relationships with war, grief, history, industry, faith, and one another.

〉〉〉 **Jean Cannon** is the Literary Collections Research Associate at the Harry Ransom Center. She received a Ph.D. from the English Department at The University of Texas at Austin, where she specialized in the British and American literature of the First World War. Cannon has worked extensively in book publishing and advertising and as a freelance writer and editor. She is co-curator of the Ransom Center exhibition *The World at War, 1914–1918.*

Soldiers

‹‹‹ FACING PAGE
Maurice Neumont
(French, 1868–1930)
"On ne passe pas! 1914–1918," 1918
LITHOGRAPH

This poster reads, "They shall not pass! 1914–1918. Twice I have held my ground and was victorious on the Marne. Civilian, my brother, the underhanded offensive of the white peace will assault you in turn. Like me, you need to hold your ground and triumph, be strong and clever. Beware of Boche hypocrisy." During the war various parties intermittently proposed a "white peace," a peace without victor or vanquished.

›››

Keystone View Company
Scene near the British supply base at Basra, Mesopotamia, not dated
GELATIN SILVER PRINT STEREOGRAPH

As soon as the Ottoman Empire entered the war in 1914, the British moved to protect and control oil reserves in Persia and Mesopotamia. British forces quickly took Basra, in present-day Iraq, but were unable to capture Baghdad until 1917. Winston Churchill described the British invasion of Mesopotamia: "[I]nstead of thrusting at Constantinople, the heart of Turkey . . . we began our attack from her fingertips upward." He also noted that "by 1918 seven British and Indian divisions, composing an army of two hundred and seventy thousand men (exclusive of followers), were operating in Mesopotamia."

⌃⌃
Christina Broom
(British, 1862–1939)
Families saying farewell to soldiers headed for active service in France, 1914
GELATIN SILVER PRINT

London street photographer Christina Broom documented the mobilization of British troops following Britain's declaration of war against Germany at midnight on August 4, 1914.

The British Parliamentary Recruiting Committee
"Step into Your Place," 1915
LITHOGRAPH

Before introducing conscription in May 1916, Great Britain was the only major European nation to rely on a volunteer army. This 1915 recruiting poster encourages all classes of British society to enlist; miners and aristocrats alike "step into [their] place" in the line of identical "Tommies" marching off to war. Though class distinctions were upheld by the British army, the high fatality rate among young subalterns necessitated that men from the ranks be promoted to officer class. Many of these "temporary gentlemen" would later lead the postwar labor strikes that shook the foundation of British socio-economics in the 1920s.

››› FACING PAGE, TOP

Abel Faivre
(French, 1867–1945)
"On les aura! [We'll get them!]," 1916
LITHOGRAPH

One of the most famous French posters of a *poilu* from the war features the quotation from an order to the troops by General Philippe Pétain (1856–1951) on April 10, 1916. French soldiers called themselves *poilu*, or "hairy." It was perhaps a reference to the macho qualities of a hairy man.

››› FACING PAGE, BOTTOM

Ellsworth Young
(American, 1866–1952)
"Remember Belgium—Buy Bonds—Fourth Liberty Loan," 1918
LITHOGRAPH

The exaggeration of German atrocities in Belgium was a propaganda staple throughout the war. Although the suffering of the Belgian civilian population is unquestionable, charges of widespread murder and mutilation appear to have been greatly overstated. It is estimated that approximately 6,400 civilians were intentionally killed by German troops in occupied Belgium and France during the war. Similarly, the burning of the university library of Louvain and the destruction of the Rheims cathedral convinced propagandists that Germany was against culture and religion, and some of the devastation wrought by the Allies was blamed on German soldiers.

New York Journal-American
Canadian soldiers entering No Man's Land, not dated
GELATIN SILVER PRINT

Photographs documenting forward attacks in World War I are scarce. This image, remarkable for its proximity to advancing soldiers, shows a Canadian regiment going "over the top" into No Man's Land. Because the photograph shows soldiers who may have been wounded or killed as the photograph was taken, it most likely would have been censored during wartime. This photograph appeared in a *New York Journal-American* feature a decade after the war's end.

Charles Fouqueray
(French, 1869–1956)
"African Army and Colonial Troop Day
[Zouave troops, Algeria]," 1917
LITHOGRAPH

Fouqueray was the official artist of the Naval and Colonial Ministries.

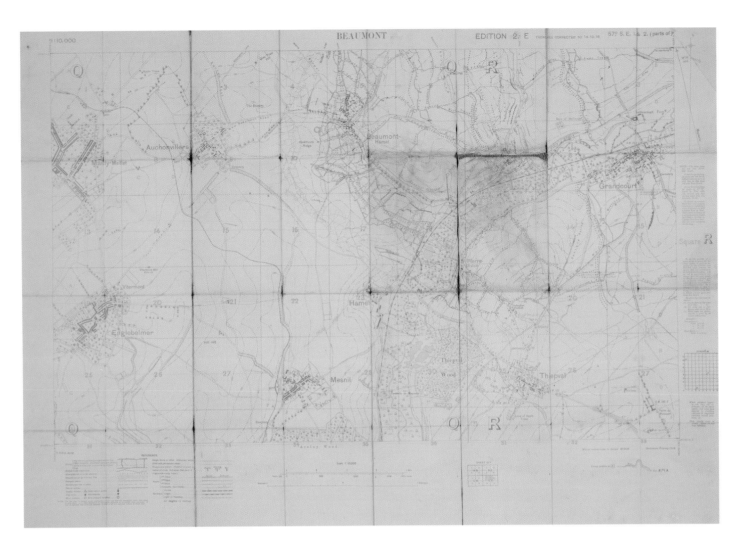

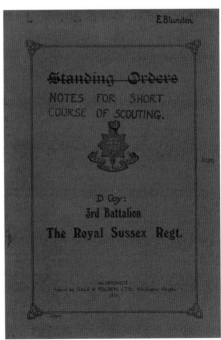

Trench map of the Beaumont-Hamel sector of the Western Front
ca. 1917

Lieutenant Edmund Blunden (1896–1974), a cartographer for the British army, annotated this map to show a winding trench known to soldiers as "Jacob's Ladder." Maps had to be updated continually, as the shelling of the Western Front quickly decimated known landmarks and obliterated buildings and roads. Between 1914 and 1918 the field survey and cartographic units of the British army published approximately 34 million such maps of the sectors of the Western Front.

Edmund Blunden's maps and lesson plans from a course on scouting in No Man's Land
ca. 1917

Night raids across No Man's Land were among the most dangerous assignments. Going "on patrol," especially on moonlit nights, left soldiers open targets for snipers. Though soldiers going on trench raids would camouflage their faces with burnt cork, No Man's Land brought great risk of death or capture. Poet Arthur Graeme West (1891–1917) wrote that night patrols were "a dangerous business, and most repulsive on account of the smells and appearances of the heaps of dead men that lie unburied."

George Nathaniel Nash
(British, b. 1888)
**Armenian refugees, many of whom died
on the road, May 1918**
GELATIN SILVER PRINTS

As a condition of the Treaty of Brest-Litovsk signed by the Central powers and Bolshevik Russia in March 1918, all Russian troops began to pull back from any territorial gains they had made in the Ottoman Empire during the war. On May 30, 1918, British Lieutenant George Nathaniel Nash, stationed as an artillery officer and translator in Russia from 1917 to 1919, wrote in his diary, "The state of the Georgian Road from Tiflis to Vladikavkaz must be appalling. It is just one long line of Armenian refugees—many on foot & their sufferings must have been intense, to say nothing of the numerous robberies. Each night at Kazbek about 3,000 refugees slept in the open waiting for the dawn to continue their journey. Many of them were ill & there were 2 cases of small pox in the hotel while I was there. I have read & heard much of Kazbek & I must confess it is a beautiful mountain—but as long as I live I don't wish to see it again."

By the time Nash encountered the Armenians fleeing from Erzurum, the Ottoman Turks had systematically massacred more than 1 million of them, either directly or through detention and deportation in deplorably inhumane conditions.

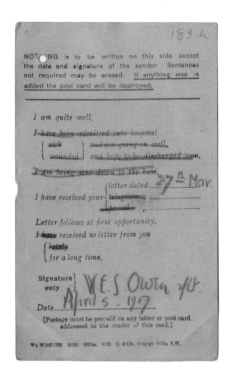

A standard British Army Field Service postcard from Wilfred Owen to his mother, Susan Owen
April 5, 1917

Letters sent by soldiers from the front lines were often heavily censored by commanding officers. The British army encouraged troops to send Field Service postcards, which offered friends and relatives scripted information about the soldier but no mention of his actual whereabouts. Soldier-poet Wilfred Owen (1893–1918) developed a code system to work around the army's form letter. Owen's double strikeout of "I am being sent down to base" indicated that he was headed to the front lines. Fearing that his mother might misread this secret system of communication and worry unduly, on October 29, 1918, Owen wrote to her, "I don't want to send Field Cards in case you suppose they mean in the Line. In future . . . a F. Card will be no proof that I am actually there." He assured his mother he was not headed toward battle. Shortly after writing the letter, Owen's battalion was moved to the front line of the Sambre-Oise Canal, where nine days later he was killed.

≪≪ FACING PAGE, TOP

New York Journal-American
Members of the 369th Infantry Division,
ca. 1917
GELATIN SILVER PRINT

The U.S. Army's 369th Infantry Division, known as
the "Harlem Hellfighters," was organized in 1913 and
became the first African American regiment to serve
with the Allied Expeditionary Force in France in 1917.
Attached to the French army, the 369th saw heavy
fighting in the Battles of the Marne and Meuse-
Argonne and suffered nearly 1,500 casualties. Their
regimental band, which played jazz, became famous
throughout Europe. In the postwar period, the 369th
frequently paraded the streets of New York, remind-
ing citizens of the sacrifices made by African Americans in service to the nation.

≪≪ FACING PAGE, BOTTOM

Unidentified photographer
1st Russian Women's Battalion of Death,
not dated
GELATIN SILVER PRINT

In June 1917 the highly decorated peasant-soldier
Maria Bochkareva (1889–1920) (bottom row, second
from left) was given permission to form a battalion
of women to fight in the upcoming Russian offensive, "to serve as an example to the army and lead
the men into battle." Unfortunately, it had just the
opposite effect. Although the Women's Battalion of
Death fought bravely and incurred 80 percent casualties as they successfully beat back the Germans,
their momentum evaporated when the supporting
troops meant to relieve them refused to advance.

Keystone View Company
Warfare in the Tropics—British Troops in pursuit of the enemy in German East Africa, not dated
GELATIN SILVER PRINT STEREOGRAPH

It has been argued that the first shots of the war were fired in Africa against a German wireless station in
Togoland. In German East Africa (present-day Burundi, Rwanda, and part of Tanzania), General Paul von Lettow-
Vorbeck (1870–1964) and his Schutztruppe eluded the British, under the command of Lieutenant General Jan
Christiaan Smuts (1870–1950), for four years with a comparatively small force. In contrast to the trench warfare
of Europe, combat in Africa typically consisted of guerrilla warfare and lightning cavalry raids. This photograph
shows the "soldiers of the British Expedition under General Smuts fording the Ruva River, German East Africa."

⌃⌃

Lucien Jonas
(French, 1880–1947)
"African Army and Colonial Troop Day," 1917
LITHOGRAPH

Approximately 500,000 colonial troops served in the French army, and about 14 percent of them were killed. Hundreds of thousands more came to France to work in the war factories. Many of the representations of the colonial soldiers evoke stereotypes of race and culture. One purpose of these posters was to reinforce the benefits of French colonialism; the French people were no longer alone in their fight because they had colonial resources to come to their aid.

The artist Lucien Jonas was mobilized in December 1914 and produced thousands of images from the front lines. He was awarded the Légion d'honneur.

⌃⌃

Lucien Jonas
(French, 1880–1947)
"Compagnie Algérienne," 1918
LITHOGRAPH

One of the only posters to illustrate colonial troop home life, its message is that subscribing to this national war loan "will hasten his return with victory."

New York Journal-American

Scottish soldiers wearing gas masks, not dated

GELATIN SILVER PRINT

During World War I, nineteenth-century military traditions and tactics gave way to twentieth-century industrialized warfare. In this photograph, the traditional, kilted uniform of the Scottish army stands in sharp contrast to the soldiers' gas masks.

Women in Wartime

⟨⟨⟨ FACING PAGE

E. J. Kealey
(nationality and dates unknown)
"Women of Britain Say—GO!," 1915
LITHOGRAPH

This poster is one of the most iconic images of the First World War. Mass-produced by the British Parliamentary Recruiting Committee and pasted onto walls and kiosks throughout England, it is indicative of the increasingly sophisticated strategies the British government used to encourage enlistment. While the poster shows British women and children needing protection, it also encourages them to press their husbands and brothers into service for king and country. The British War Office found propaganda directed toward women particularly successful, especially after British newspapers reported that the German army enacted ghastly atrocities against women and children when it invaded Belgium in 1914.

⟩⟩⟩

George Mather Richards
(American, 1880–1958)
"Oh Boy! That's the Girl!," ca. 1917
LITHOGRAPH

In 1917 the Salvation Army "lassies" became famous for their "Doughnuts for Doughboys" campaign. Approximately 250 women set up kitchens in abandoned huts near the front lines and provided food and first aid to weary soldiers. Ensign Margaret Sheldon and Adjutant Helen Purviance of the Salvation Army are credited with first serving doughnuts to soldiers, and the treat was instantly popular. The women became known as the "Doughnut Girls" and were celebrated in popular songs and posters.

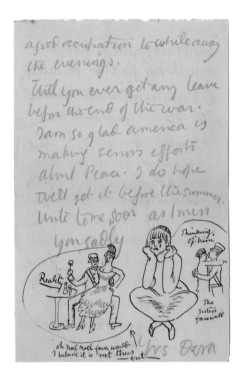

Letter from Dora Carrington to Noel Carrington
not dated

The Bloomsbury artist Dora Carrington (1893–1932) had three brothers who served in World War I. Sam, the eldest, was severely shell shocked. Teddy, her middle and favorite brother, was killed during the Battle of the Somme. Noel, the youngest, was wounded in the elbow by a German sniper and nearly lost his arm. Carrington corresponded with her brothers faithfully throughout the war, often including humorous drawings. Although a committed pacifist, Carrington, in solidarity with her brothers, involved herself in activities dedicated to improving the morale of soldiers. Early in the war, Carrington acted in a series of theatrical entertainments organized by actress Lena Ashwell (1872–1957). In 1917 Ashwell, who sent 25 theater troupes to France, was awarded the Order of the British Empire, one of the nation's most prestigious service awards.

Letter from Freya Stark to Flora Stark
August 10, 1917

The British writer Freya Stark (1893–1993), one of the most famous explorers of her generation, served as a Voluntary Aid Detachment nurse on the Italian front. In this uncensored letter to her mother, which Stark smuggled out of her field hospital, she describes the dangers of life near the artillery fire of the trenches and the difficulties of treating wounded soldiers arriving by ambulance. Stark, like nurse Catherine Barkley of Ernest Hemingway's *A Farewell to Arms* (1929), helped attend to the more than 20,000 wounded Italian soldiers who were evacuated from the Austro-Italian front following the Battle of Caporetto in October–November 1917. The battle signified the first successful, widespread assault carried out with poison gas. In one day the Italian army lost 11,000 men to the German offensive.

Gordon Conway
(American, 1894–1956)
Cover illustration for *Vanity Fair*, 1918
GOUACHE AND INK ON PAPER

Dallas-born artist and costume designer Gordon Conway's drawings of socialites and flappers for *Vanity Fair* captured the changing roles of women in early twentieth-century America. This colorful painting of a First World War nurse was rejected by the magazine but later used by the Red Cross for its recruitment posters.

<<<

Christina Broom
(British, 1862–1939)
Newly deputized policewomen, 1916
GELATIN SILVER PRINT

As more and more men were mobilized for the global war effort, women were recruited for service on the home fronts. Between 1914 and 1918 more than 1,000 women were deputized for police work in London. These policewomen became known for their efforts to curtail "khaki fever": the loosening of morals and increasing promiscuity brought about by wartime conditions. In an effort to stop indecent behavior, policewomen were assigned to patrol parks, where they separated embracing couples and arrested prostitutes. The March 1918 Defense of the Realm Act (DORA) allowed policewomen to detain and prosecute any venereally infected woman accused of having sexual relations with a member of the armed forces.

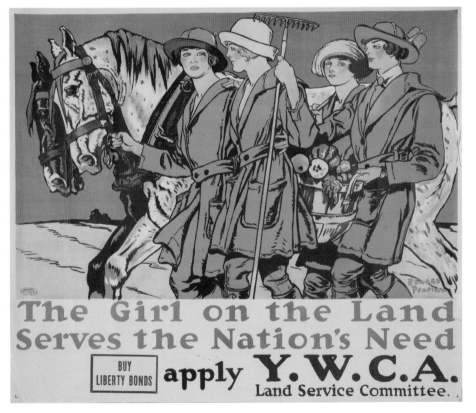

<<<

Edward Penfield
(American, 1866–1925)
"The Girl on the Land Serves the Nation's Need,"
1918
LITHOGRAPH

The Women's Land Army of America (WLAA) was organized in 1917 to plow fields, drive tractors, and plant and harvest crops. Developed by a consortium of civic groups, women's colleges, gardening clubs, the YWCA, and suffragette societies, the "farmerettes" grew to a force of 20,000 and became symbols of women's liberation and support of the war effort. Though many male farmers were initially skeptical of "land lassies" who wore pants and military tunics and demanded the same wages as men, the WLAA nonetheless successfully alleviated the extreme wartime farm labor shortage brought on by enlistment. One of their popular slogans was "Joan of Arc left the soil to save France. We're going back to the soil to save America."

Clarence Frederick Underwood
(American, 1871–1929)
"Back Our Girls Over There," ca. 1917
LITHOGRAPH

The American Signal Corps Female Telephone Operators Unit, known as the "Hello Girls," operated telephone switchboards in France from late 1917 until the end of the war. General Pershing, who organized the Hello Girls, demanded that the switchboard operators be bilingual, have college educations, be at least 25 years old, and be single. Of the nearly 7,000 volunteers, 450 were chosen; the vast majority of these were former employees of the American Telephone and Telegraph (AT&T) Company. The women received military training, wore uniforms, and were subject to the same rules and regulations as male Signal Corps soldiers.

Though chief operator Grace Banker received the Distinguished Service Medal in 1918 for her war work, returning Hello Girls were denied official veteran status. Only after tireless campaigning by former Hello Girl Merle Egan Anderson was the status of the group changed from civilian volunteer to certified member of the military. In 1977 President Jimmy Carter signed a bill instating former Hello Girls as official First World War veterans, and the 50 who were still living at the time received honorable discharges, belated by 60 years.

Adolph Treidler
(American, 1886–1981)
"For Every Fighter a Woman Worker," 1918
LITHOGRAPH

Millions of female laborers took enlisted men's places in munitions factories between 1917 and 1918. Women worked long hours at an average of two-thirds the typical wage for men. Though leading labor unions opposed employing women in munitions factories, war-relief groups such as the United War Work campaign aggressively advocated war work for women.

LEROY. — La Receveuse de Tramway. — The Guard.

LEROY. — L'Heure du Communiqué. — The Communiqué.

Maurice Leroy
(French, 1885–1973)
The Tramway Conductor, 1917

This series of images illustrates the changing roles of women, and their stereo-types, during the First World War. Initially, the French government did not mobilize women for the war effort other than as nurses. By the summer of 1916, however, all the available men were needed at the Somme, and the government began actively recruiting women to work in war industries. Unfortunately, this change in status did not last into peacetime. Women who did not immediately quit their new jobs after the return of the *poilus* were sometimes accused of war profiteering.

Maurice Leroy
(French, 1885–1973)
Time for the Mail Delivery, 1917

Writers

Unidentified photographer
Siegfried Sassoon in uniform, not dated
GELATIN SILVER PRINT

»»

Manuscript of Siegfried Sassoon's poem "The General"
1918

Poet Siegfried Sassoon (1886–1967) became well known during the war for the satirical verses he wrote from the Western Front. Many of his poems blamed the high command of the British army for ineptitude, lack of compassion for the lower ranks, and bungled offensives that cost thousands of young lives. On July 27, 1917, Sassoon published a formal declaration against the generals and politicians responsible for running the war, stating that he believed "the war [was] being deliberately prolonged by those who have the power to end it."

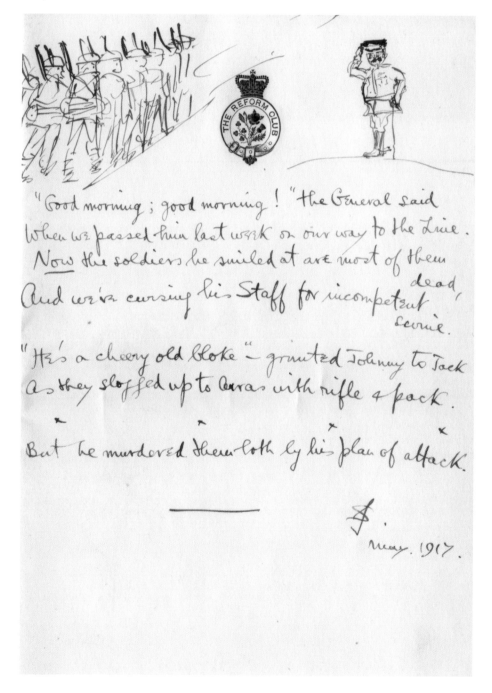

Unidentified photographer
Rupert Brooke, ca. 1914
GELATIN SILVER PRINT

›››
Manuscript of Rupert Brooke's poem "1914"

At the time of his death, Rupert Brooke (1887–1915) was considered England's foremost—and most dashing—young poet. Brooke's literary stardom is credited to a series of war sonnets he published after witnessing the fall of Antwerp. The sonnet "1914," Brooke's most popular poem, became synonymous with the British cause, and war supporters quoted his depiction of Flanders as a "foreign field that is for ever England" extensively. When Brooke died from septicemia en route to the Gallipoli campaign in 1915, his death was mourned throughout Britain. Winston Churchill wrote Brooke's obituary for the London *Times*, hailing the lost poet as "all that one could wish England's noblest sons to be."

In his last letter to his friend and literary executor Edward Marsh (1872–1953), Brooke wrote, "You must decide everything about publication. Don't print too much bad stuff. . . . I wish I'd written more. I've been such a failure." The posthumously published *1914 and Other Poems* sold in the tens of thousands and made Brooke a lasting icon of the "Generation of 1914."

I

1914.

Peace —

Now, God be thanked, who has matched us with His hour,
And caught our youth, & wakened us from sleeping,
With hand made sure, clear eye, & sharpened power,
To turn, as swimmers into cleanness leaping,
Glad from a world grown old & cold & weary,
Leave the sick hearts whom honour could not move,
And half-men, & their dirty songs & dreary,
And all the little emptiness of love!

Oh, we, who have known shame, we have found release there,
Where there's no hurt, no ill, but sleep has mending;
Naught broken save this body, lost but breath;
Nothing to shake the laughing heart's long peace there
But only agony, and that has ending;
And the worst friend & enemy is but Death.

Unidentified photographer
Ernest Hemingway, ca. 1917
GELATIN SILVER PRINT

Ernest Hemingway (1899–1961) joined the Red Cross Ambulance Corps in December 1917 at age 18 after being rejected by the U.S. Army for defective vision. He served as a driver on the Italian front. In July 1918 a trench mortar exploded three feet from Hemingway, and his legs were lacerated by shrapnel in 227 places. He received the Silver Medal of Valor for carrying another injured soldier to a field hospital during the attack, and the story appeared in newspapers in the United States and abroad.

Hemingway wrote his family that the publicity was "the next best thing to getting killed and reading your own obituary." More important, while convalescing in a war hospital in Milan, Hemingway met and fell in love with Agnes von Kurowsky, a Red Cross nurse who would become the model for nurse Catherine Barkley in *A Farewell to Arms* (1929).

William Faulkner's sketch of a Royal Air Force cadet
1918

In 1918, when 20-year-old William Faulkner (1897–1962) enlisted in the Canadian Royal Air Force, he wrote to his parents: "At the rate I am living now, I will never be able to make anything of myself, but with this business I'll be fixed up after the war is over." Instead of finding aerial adventure, Faulkner found himself cleaning airplanes. Bored and disappointed, in letters home Faulkner invented romantic stories about flights he never made and boasted about skills he never acquired. In an August 11, 1918, letter to his mother, Faulkner includes a drawing: "My new uniform will be like this." Yet Faulkner never wore the uniform in service. He was one week short of completing ground school when the Armistice was declared.

Book jacket of the unexpurgated American edition of Erich Maria Remarque's *All Quiet on the Western Front*

1930

German ex-serviceman Erich Maria Remarque's controversial *All Quiet on the Western Front* created an international sensation when it was published in 1929. Many readers, including veterans, thought that Remarque's novel sensationalized the events of the war and presented a one-sided portrait of trench life as unremittingly filthy, brutal, filled with horrors, and overseen by incompetent officers.

The first American edition of *All Quiet on the Western Front* was expurgated by publisher Little, Brown at the request of the Book-of-the-Month Club, which thought that Remarque's original text—including a long section dedicated to a battalion's visit to a camp latrine—would repel the average reader.

The book fared far worse in Germany, where it was burned publicly by Nazis, who claimed that the novel represented treason against the fatherland. In 1938 Remarque's German citizenship was revoked. Remarque lived in exile for the rest of his life and became a naturalized U.S. citizen in 1947.

A first edition of Frederic Manning's *Her Privates We*

(London: Peter Davies, 1930)

Australian writer and poet Frederic Manning (1882–1935) fought on the Western Front as a low-ranking infantry soldier and became one of the few privates to publish an influential war book based on his experiences. Manning's anonymously published *The Middle Parts of Fortune* (1929) tells the story of soldiers of the ranks during the Battle of the Somme, with dialog written in colorful—and often blasphemous—vernacular and slang. Following a 520-volume print run of the controversial unexpurgated version of the book, Manning's publisher, Peter Davies, changed the title to *Her Privates We* (both titles are taken from the dialog of Rosencrantz and Guildenstern in *Hamlet*) and advertised the author as "Private 19022." Only in 1943 was authorship officially and posthumously credited to Manning. His book was hailed by former soldiers. Ernest Hemingway called it "the finest and noblest book of men in war" and claimed to read Manning's book once a year so he would not forget "how things really were."

》》》 FACING PAGE, TOP LEFT AND RIGHT

Letter from Guillaume Apollinaire to Louise de Coligny-Châtillon, "Lou"

April 18, 1915

》》》 FACING PAGE, BOTTOM LEFT

Guillaume Apollinaire's poem "La nuit d'Avril, 1915"

Poet Guillaume Apollinaire (1880–1918) was born Wilhelm Apollinaris de Kostrowitzky in Italy to a Polish mother and an Italian father, yet he fought on behalf of the French during the First World War. Apollinaire served as a corporal of the 38th Regiment, 43rd Artillery and wrote this poem while advancing to the front lines. This manuscript draft has several variations from the final published version.

Apollinaire joined his regiment while in Nice. There he met Louise de Coligny-Châtillon (1881–1963), a divorcée volunteering as a nurse, who was also one of the first female French pilots, and Apollinaire fell deeply under her spell. In April 1915 Apollinaire, frustrated with his relationship with "Lou," quit officer training school and asked to be sent to the front. This letter contains a 32-line poem beginning "Mon Lou, ma chérie, je t'envoie aujourd'hui la première pervenche" (My Lou, my darling, today I am sending you the first periwinkle). Lou inspired many of Apollinaire's greatest poems, and he dedicated "La nuit d'Avril, 1915" (The Night of April, 1915) to her.

》》》 FACING PAGE, BOTTOM RIGHT

Jean Hugo

(French, 1894–1984)
Portrait of Guillaume Apollinaire, not dated
PEN AND INK

In March 1916, while reading a newspaper, Apollinaire was hit in his temple by a piece of shell shrapnel that pierced his helmet. The wound required trepanation, and his scar healed in the shape of a star on his forehead. Ironically, the wound occurred the same year as the publication of Apollinaire's work *Le poète assassiné.*

Artist Jean Hugo, grandson of the French author Victor Hugo (1802–1885), was a sergeant in the 36th Infantry Division. He was wounded in battle and served with distinction. The 36th was one of the divisions that mutinied in May 1917. Disgusted with his men, Hugo requested a transfer, which was accelerated by his mother's friendship with French President Raymond Poincaré (1860–1934), and he spent the rest of the war as a translator for the American troops.

Le 18 Avril 1915

Mon petit chéri, il est 6 heures, le vaguemestre vient de venir et n'avait pas de lettre de toi. Je suis triste à penser que tu peux être malheureuse, mon très cher amour. J'ai fini ma journée, je lis un roman à 13 sous, les Milliers de trappeurs. Je pense que ton déménagement est fini, que tu vas faire gentiment dodo et que tout va redevenir rose si le papa ne tarde pas trop... Que dans ton dodo, tu vas faire de jolis rêves, où il sera peut-être même un peu question de moi. Je vous embrasse gentiment et vois quand tu te coucheras j'irai encore t'embrasser calinement puis je te bercerai comme ma gosse chérie, et quand tu dormiras je te veillerai en t'embrassant longtemps, doucement, sans t'éveiller. Je te dirai aussi, ma très jolie, de très jolies, de très tendres choses, tout bas à l'oreille sous tes jolis cheveux dont j'adore la couleur sanglante, émouvante; et que je te dirai si gentiment si tendrement fera partie de tes jolis rêves, ma chérie. Je te dirai surtout: je t'aime, je t'aime, je t'aime encore je suis à toi malgré toi pour toujours et je te prendrai toute, toute, pantelante dans un beau rêve ou dans nos adorations. Je te prendrai toute et ferai surgir rose avec toi que tu es le petit garçon joli dans ce poème...

Mon Lou, ma chérie je t'envoie aujourd'hui la première pervenche, cueillie dans la forêt où s'organise des luttes entre les hommes. Il s'ennuient d'être tout seuls, tous femme, fait bien tes amours te dérange depuis si longtemps qu'ils sont loin de tout de revoir à jamais parlé. Et parfois je suis tenté de leur montrer ton portrait pour que ces pauvres morts

Respecteraient en voyant la fleur

Ce que c'est que la beauté

Mais elle n'est pour eux, c'est pour moi seul

---

moi seul ai droit de parler à ce portrait qui pâlit
À ce portrait qui s'efface

Je te regarde parfois longtemps, une heure simplement
Et je regarde aussi les 2 petits portraits minuscules
Mon cœur
La bataille des dieux dure toujours
La nuit est venue

Quelle triste chanson fond dans la nuit profonde
Les obus qui tournaient comme de petits mondes

M'entends-tu donc mon cœur, et ton âme bien nôtre
Peut-elle du bonheur dont ma tête est vouée!
J'y joindrai bien aussi de ces beaux myrtes verts,
Couronne des amants qui ne sont pas pervers,
En attendant encor que le chêne me donne
Sa guerrière couronne.

Et quand te reverrai-je, ô toi, ma bien-aimée
Reverrai-je Paris et sa tête humaine
Trembler les soirs de brume autour des réverbères
Reverrai-je Paris et les toucher sous les voilettes
Les petits pieds rapides des femmes inconnues
La tour de Saint Germain des prés
La fontaine du Luxembourg
Et toi mon adoré, mon amour que j'adore
Toi mon très cher amour?

Je t'aime tant jolie
tout gentiment
Mon joli petit Lou
et je t'embrasse
Lui

La nuit d'Avril 1915

À L. de C.P.

Le ciel est étoilé par les obus des Boches
La forêt merveilleuse où je vis donne un bal
La mitrailleuse joue un air à triples croches
Mais avez-vous le mot? Eh! oui le mot fatal
Aux créneaux Aux créneaux laissez là les pioches

Comme un astre éperdu qui cherche ses saisons
Cœur obus éclaté tu sifflais ta romance
Et tes mille soleils ont vidé les caissons
Que les dieux de mes yeux remplissent en silence
        Nous nous aimons
    O Vie et nous nous agaçons

Les obus miaulaient un amour à mourir
Un amour qui se meurt est plus doux que les autres
Mon souffle nage au fleuve où le sang va tarir
Les obus miaulaient entends chanter les nôtres
Pourpre amour salué par ceux qui vont périr

Le printemps tout mouillé la veilleuse l'attaque
Il pleut mon âme il pleut mais il pleut des yeux morts
— Ulysse! que de jours pour rentrer dans Ithaque —
Couche-toi sur la paille et songe un beau remords
Qui par effet de l'art soit aphrodisiaque

Mais, orgues aux fêtes de la
        paille où tu dors
L'hymne de l'avenir est
        paradisiaque

Guillaume
Apollinaire

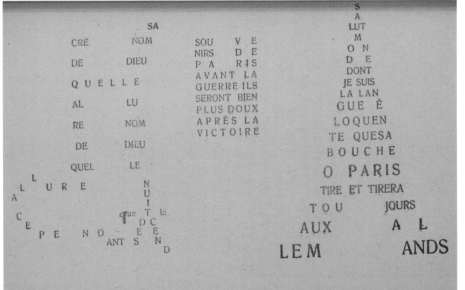

‹‹‹

Calligrammes. Poèmes de la paix et de la guerre (1913–1916)
(Paris: Mercure de France, 1918)

Apollinaire, weakened by his head wound, succumbed to the Spanish flu on November 9, 1918, just days before the end of the war. His last words, as reported by his friends, were "I want to live; I want to live; I have so many things to do."

This collection of Apollinaire's poems, in which the typeface and special arrangement of the words play a significant role in each poem's meaning, is subtitled *Poems of Peace and War (1913–1916)*.

Artists

〉〉〉

Eric Gill
(British, 1882–1940)
Westward Ho!, 1921
WOOD ENGRAVING ON PAPER

This image of a war-weary soldier was engraved
by celebrated illustrator and sculptor Eric Gill, who
based his design on a drawing rendered by war
veteran and memoirist David Jones (1895–1974).
Jones, a protégé of Gill's, produced this image
of a trudging infantryman as the two artists were
designing the base of the Trumpington War
Memorial, near Cambridge. After serving as an
apprentice to Gill in the 1920s, Jones published his
prose-poem recollection of his experiences on the
Western Front, titled *In Parenthesis* (1937).

"L'escalier de Chambord" je
monte en sens inverse avec
des mufles + rouge qui ne
comprennent rien à leur mission
et transportent sur le front leurs
antiritas.
Le pays de front console. C'est
un sanatorium de gentillesse
camarade — le cœur qui engraisse
comme la figure et les Zouaves
valent mieux que des rues.

— Dunes et tempêtes — J'ai pensé
à vous toute ma nuit de Noël aux
premières lignes. Silence de
Bethléem, odeur de crèche, fièvre
de mitraille, tirailleurs debout
et graves comme les mages,
grosses étoiles d'aluminium qui elles
règlent les tirs).

— On croise la nuit sur les routes
des ânes, des indigènes, des
machines étranges — Bible et

apocalypse.

— Les obus tombent sur des
usines — on les écoute ou les
regarde avec une stupeur toujours
neuve — homme splendide
J'ai vu des capitaines pleurer
comme des enfants et des
enfants rudes comme de
vieux capitaines.

Dîtes à la colombe à côté
jardin, qu'elle annonce la
fin du déluge.

Tendre respect.   Jean

Jean Cocteau

(French, 1889–1963)

L'U DADA, ca. 1914

INK ON PAPER

© 2013 ADAGP, Paris / Avec l'aimable autorisation de M. Pierre Bergé, président du Comité Jean Cocteau

The French author and artist Jean Cocteau had already finished his illustrated picaresque novel *Le Potomak* when the war broke out. During the Battle of the Marne, he redrew some of the illustrations, adding German pointed helmets to the adversaries.

Letter from Jean Cocteau to Abbé Arthur Mugnier

December 1915

© 2013 ADAGP, Paris / Avec l'aimable autorisation de M. Pierre Bergé, président du Comité Jean Cocteau

Cocteau writes to his spiritual adviser, Abbé Mugnier (1853–1944), from the front lines at the extreme western edge of the Allied trenches: "Dunes and tempests. I thought of you the whole night of Christmas at the front lines. Silence of Bethlehem, scent of stable, cease-fire from the hail of bullets, infantrymen upright and solemn as the Wise Men, huge aluminum stars, which adjust the fire, alas."

Letter from Pablo Picasso to Henri-Pierre Roché

August 1915

© 2013 Estate of Pablo Picasso / Artists Rights Society (ARS), New York

In his letter, Picasso (1881–1973) writes to author, art dealer, and collector Roché (1879–1959): "My dear friend, Braque is wounded. That's all I know. Here is his address—Second Lieutenant Braque—Ambulance 1/18, Postal Sector 96. Perhaps with the help of your general [Malleterre] you could telegraph for news about how he is. I would be so grateful. . . . You know my friendship for Braque."

Artist Georges Braque (1882–1963), who, along with Picasso, invented Cubism, was wounded in the head in battle at Carency on May 11, 1915. He underwent trepanation surgery and temporarily lost his sight. Braque was subsequently awarded the Croix de guerre and the Légion d'honneur. After Apollinaire was wounded, a French author joked that the Germans were aiming at the heads of French artists and writers.

>>> TOP LEFT

International Film Service Inc. / *New York Journal-American*

James Montgomery Flagg painting in Midtown Manhattan, 1918

GELATIN SILVER PRINT

Artist James Montgomery Flagg (1877–1960) is best remembered for his iconic "I Want YOU for U.S. Army" poster, in which he modeled the face of Uncle Sam on his own. An ardent advocate for American recruitment, in this July 1918 photograph Flagg paints an enormous canvas of the "Tell That to the Marines!" poster outside the New York Public Library. Flagg hoped his public performance would increase enlistment numbers.

>>> TOP RIGHT

James Montgomery Flagg

(American, 1877–1960)

"Tell That to the Marines!," ca. 1918

LITHOGRAPH

>>> BOTTOM LEFT

William Rothenstein

(British, 1872–1945)

Portrait of Eric Kennington, 1918

PASTEL

© Estate of Sir William Rothenstein/ Bridgeman Art Library

Eric Kennington (1888–1960) served alongside William Rothenstein as an official war artist for the British army on the Western Front during 1917–1918. In the years following the war, Kennington became well known as the designer of both the Battersea Park memorial in London and the memorial to Allied forces in Soissons, France. He also achieved fame with his illustrations for T. E. Lawrence's *Seven Pillars of Wisdom* (1926).

>>> BOTTOM RIGHT

John Thomason

(American, 1893–1944)

Sketches of soldiers, ca. 1917

Artist John Thomason was born in Huntsville, Texas, attended The University of Texas at Austin from 1912 to 1913, and after working briefly as a writer and illustrator for the *Houston Chronicle*, joined the U.S. Marine Corps in 1917. Throughout the war he sketched the everyday lives of soldiers and collected these drawings in his war narrative, *Fix Bayonets!* (1926). The book was hailed by such newspapers as the London *Times*, which concluded, "No book which we can recall that has for subject the actual fighting man in the Great War, has appeared to us to equal this. The drawings match the prose."

Animals

>>>

Fortunino Matania
(British, b. Italy, 1881–1963)
"Help the Horse to Save the Soldier," ca. 1917
LITHOGRAPH

The subterranean landscape of trench warfare dramatically changed the role of horses in wartime. Instead of leading cavalry charges, horses were relegated largely to hauling supplies behind the lines. Horses also became the target of the world's first organized campaign of biological warfare, conducted by a German-American doctor named Anton Dilger (1884–1918). Dilger, who was living in Germany and treating wounded civilians at the start of the war, became incensed that the United States, a declared neutral nation, continued to deliver huge shipments of horses to the Allies, and he offered to help the Germans stop them. The German government supplied Dilger with pure strains of anthrax and glanders, which Dilger produced in a basement laboratory in Maryland. He then paid stevedores in Virginia to administer these to horses waiting on the docks to be delivered to Britain and France. His sabotage campaign was successful, and equine pandemics broke out in Allied horse stables, killing thousands of animals. Dilger came under suspicion of espionage by the FBI and fled to Mexico and then Spain, where he died of influenza. Meanwhile, the German government found a more effective means of stopping American shipments of horses to the Allies. In 1916 they introduced a concentrated submarine campaign against U.S. ships carrying livestock. Overall, nearly 7,000 horses and mules died after their transport ships were torpedoed by German submarines.

New York Journal-American
A French infantryman deploying pigeons,
ca. 1917
GELATIN SILVER PRINT

This image illustrates the method of transferring carrier pigeon messages from the trenches to base camps located several miles behind the front lines. An officer in the trenches would write a brief message on a small piece of paper, place it in a slender aluminum tube, and attach the tube to the leg of the pigeon to be released. If the pigeon evaded danger and returned to its coop, a bell would sound, and a member of the Signal Corps would remove the message and forward it by telegram, telephone, or personal messenger. The constant shelling of telephone lines in the trenches, combined with the high success rate of the "pigeon post," made carrier pigeons an essential component of army life. By the end of the war, the British army alone had 100,000 trained birds at its dispatch. Because carrier pigeons could fly distances of almost 200 miles at more than 60 miles per hour, they were also a favorite method of communication between ships at sea and military units on land.

A pigeon named Cher Ami became a prized pet of the American infantry after saving the lives of trapped soldiers during the Battle of Argonne. When Cher Ami died of wounds just months after the end of the war, he was widely mourned by veterans and awarded the French Croix de guerre for his heroic efforts in the Battle of Verdun. Cher Ami's taxidermied remains are on display at the Smithsonian Institution's National Museum of American History.

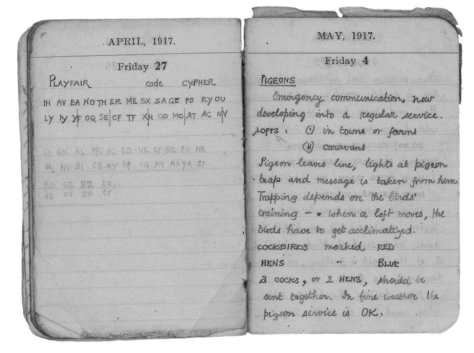

Edmund Blunden's war diary, with notes about carrier pigeons
1917

While employing the telephone in battlefield communications for the first time in World War I, armies also relied heavily on a much older form of communication: the "pigeon post." Carrier pigeons—because of their small size, dull coloring, speed, and ability to fly above tear gas—could often navigate under heavy artillery fire much better than human dispatch runners. The majority of birds used in the war were donated by civilian pigeon fanciers to military Signal Corps, who trained the pigeons to fly from the trenches to home coops kept at a stationary headquarters behind the lines. Both Allied and Central powers trained hawks to hunt the pigeons and intercept messages. Edmund Blunden's war diary contains notes about the care of the birds and the successful sending of "pigeongrams." Blunden records that pigeons should be kept hungry so that they fly quickly to their home coop and that their transport "assault baskets" should be "kept clean and out of rats' way." On the facing page, Blunden has written a cipher for use in encoding messages.

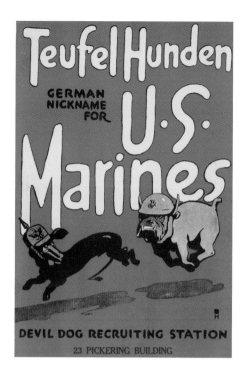

Charles Buckles Falls
(American, 1874–1959)
"Teufel Hunden—German Nickname for
U.S. Marines," 1918
LITHOGRAPH

According to U.S. Marine Corps lore, the Marine nickname "devil dog" originated in an April 1917 German army dispatch from the front lines to high command—one that described fresh American troops as *Teufel Hunden*, or "dogs from hell." Use of the slang term "devil dog" for a Marine Corps infantryman soon proliferated through the American press, usually accompanied by an image of a bulldog, the official mascot of the U.S. Marine Corps. This recruitment poster featuring a dachshund chased by a bulldog is one of the first of the Marine Corps's official uses of the "devil dog" nickname.

International News Photo /
New York Journal-American
German war dog, ca. 1916–1918
GELATIN SILVER PRINT

While American and British forces relied primarily on carrier pigeons to deliver messages at the front, the German army employed a highly trained corps of war dogs. Dogs were active in the German forces in nineteenth-century wars, and by 1900 the German army had established multiple dog-training schools that turned canines into dispatch runners. During the First World War, German dog trainers expanded the use of dogs in military action to include searching for wounded soldiers on battlefields, carrying out sentry duty and scout missions, transporting supplies, and laying signal wire from backpacks strapped to dogs' backs. Unlike pigeons (which were used only during the day), war dogs had superior night vision and became valued evening message bearers. Pigeons could fly above tear gas, however, and dogs could not, which led to the development of canine gas masks.

The Imperial German Army used approximately 30,000 war dogs during the First World War. Military dog-training programs are still a part of most major armies.

Julius Ussy Engelhard
(German, b. Indonesia, 1883–1964)
"Bolshevism Brings War, Unemployment, and Famine," 1918
LITHOGRAPH

While the Allies used ape imagery to depict the German "mad brute," German propagandists in the latter stage of the war used ape images to depict the threat of Communism. This bestial Bolshevik, armed with fangs, knife, and smoking grenade, represents the Communist as the subhuman destroyer of civilization.

Harry Ryle Hopps
(American, 1869–1937)
"Destroy This Mad Brute!," ca. 1916–1917
LITHOGRAPH

The "Mad Brute" ape of this American recruitment poster is perhaps the most notorious depiction of German militarism to emerge from the First World War. The poster references Germany's 1914 invasion of Belgium, which came to be known as the "Rape of Belgium," a propaganda term that protested both Germany's violation of Belgium's neutrality and reported German Army atrocities against women and children.

The image was so widespread and well remembered that in 1939, just five days after the invasion of Poland, Joseph Goebbels (1897–1945), the Reich Minister of Propaganda in Nazi Germany, reprinted the poster with the title "The Old Hatred—the Old Goal!" Goebbels's caption read: "When they assaulted us 25 years ago, they wrote on their rotten slanderous poster: 'Destroy this mad beast'—they meant the German people!!!"

‹‹‹

Mildred Moody
(nationality and dates unknown)
"Even a Dog Enlists, Why Not You?," ca. 1917
LITHOGRAPH

The keen hearing and eyesight of dogs made them a valuable asset to the Medical Corps and Red Cross volunteers near the front lines of battle. Because of their superior auditory sense, dogs could often anticipate—and therefore outrun—artillery shells. Medical Corps dogs were trained to enter No Man's Land at night and seek out wounded soldiers. The dogs were taught to recognize the smell of blood, check the soldier for breath, and, if the soldier was still alive, return his hat to the Medical Corps officer waiting in the front lines. By identifying the insignia on the hat, the officer would then send stretcher bearers to remove the wounded soldier at first light.

›››

August Hutaf
(American, 1874–1942)
"'Treat 'Em Rough!' / United States Tank Corps," ca. 1918
LITHOGRAPH

In 1918 the newly formed American Tank Corps adopted this belligerent black cat—usually drawn with bared fangs and claws—as its unofficial insignia. Though there are many conflicting stories about the origin of the yellow-eyed attacker, the cat and the Tank Corps slogan "Treat 'Em Rough!" were frequently painted on the armored sides of the army's much-talked-about new weaponry. One of the earliest supporters of the tank was George S. Patton (1885–1945), the first commander of the American Expeditionary Force's 1st Light Tank Battalion in France. His future commander, Dwight D. Eisenhower (1890–1969), was in Maryland during World War I, organizing the army's 1st Heavy Tank Battalion. In a memo from this time, Eisenhower wrote: "The Tank Corps, although the baby branch of the service, is a baby in name—perhaps a baby wild cat—and the slogan 'Treat 'Em Rough' will prove to be a very appreciative phrase when the kitten has grown a bit more and sharpened his claws."

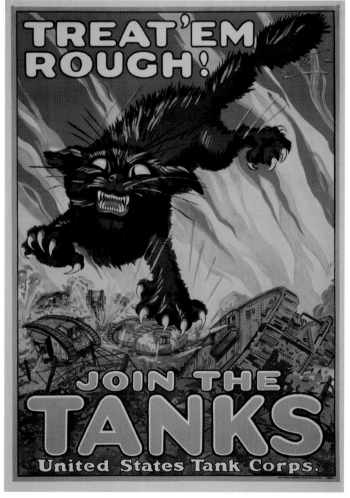

Scientists and Engineers

<<<
Maurice Neumont
(French, 1868–1930)
"Poilu's Day," December 1915
LITHOGRAPH

>>> FACING PAGE, BOTTOM
New York Journal-American
Hiram Maxim and his invention, the machine gun, not dated
GELATIN SILVER PRINT

American inventor Hiram Maxim (1840–1916), a rival of Thomas Edison (1847–1931), first patented the machine gun in 1883. After further development, it went into mass production during U.S. mobilization for the war. Maxim stated that he first got the idea for the machine gun in 1882 when a friend in Vienna told him, "Hang your chemistry and electricity! If you want to make a pile of money, invent something that will enable these Europeans to cut each other's throats with greater facility." Maxim took the advice seriously, and by the 1910s was selling machine guns to the Kaiser, the Russian Czar, and the British army. The Maxim gun, which allowed a handful of gunners to subdue masses of enemy infantry, changed the nature of modern warfare and was largely responsible for the high fatality rates on all fronts of the war.

Maxim later expressed remorse for his invention. After failing to obtain backing for medical innovations, he commented, "From the foregoing it will be seen that it is a very creditable thing to invent a killing machine, and nothing less than a disgrace to invent an apparatus to prevent human suffering."

Christina Broom
(British, 1862–1939)
Platoon of Irish Guards with machine guns,
August 1914
GELATIN SILVER PRINT

At the beginning of the war, the British army issued two machine guns, which were handled by a platoon of approximately 15 soldiers, to each of its infantry battalions. This photograph shows the machine-gun section of the Irish Guards waiting for deployment to France in August 1914 in front of "Machine Gun Shed East." The following year, the British army established a Machine Gun Corps formed of larger units of specially trained artillery soldiers.

In his memoir, *Blasting and Bombardiering*, artillery officer and artist Wyndham Lewis (1882–1957) wrote: "A gunner does not fight. He merely shells and is shelled. He discharges a large metal cylinder, aiming it by means of a delicately-adjusted mechanism, to fall at a certain spot which he cannot see, in the hope that he may kill somebody he hopes is there. . . . The gunner rarely if ever sees the enemy."

《《《
New York Journal-American
British "Blarney Castle" tank on the
Western Front, ca. 1917–1918
GELATIN SILVER PRINT

The armies of the Western Front were in a stalemate for the first three years of the war, making only minuscule infantry advances. The tank was designed by British army engineers to break the military deadlock on the Western Front. The British hoped that their new secret weapon would overwhelm the enemy with a show of technological mastery.

Tanks were first sent into action at the end of the Battle of the Somme in 1916. Though many of the 18 tanks put on the battlefield broke down, British newspapers reported their use as a wild success. In spring 1918 the British government launched a "Tank Bank" fund-raiser in which military carrier pigeon post delivered war-bond checks to tanks on display in Trafalgar Square. Citizens of London were asked to choose between "British bonds to-day or German bondage to-morrow." The War Office raised £4.5 million in the first week of the campaign.

New York Journal-American
Soldiers cutting barbed wire, date unknown
GELATIN SILVER PRINT

Trenches on both sides of the Western Front were
protected by millions of miles of barbed wire strung
on pickets, intended to entangle and halt the
progress of forward-attacking enemy soldiers. As
war continued and front lines shifted, No Man's Land
became a dense thicket of wire placed within range
of machine guns; industrial wire cutters became one
of the most valued tools of the infantry soldier. This
photograph shows American soldiers cutting a path
through barbed-wire entanglements in preparation
for an attack on German positions. The grotesque
and ghostly forms of dead bodies ensnared in
barbed wire in No Man's Land inspired the British
army euphemism of death as "hanging on the old
barbed wire."

>>>

Frank Brangwyn
(British, b. New York, 1867–1956)
"The Zeppelin Raids: The Vow of Vengeance,"
1916
LITHOGRAPH

Between 1914 and 1918 the German army made 51
zeppelin raids over England that killed 557 civilians
and caused extensive property damage. The air-
ship assaults blurred the line between the home
front and battlefront, and British propagandists
quickly exploited German attacks against women
and children to encourage enlistment. Zeppelins
were depicted as omens of a barbarous future in
which weapons of mass destruction would be turned
against civilian populations.

   At the outbreak of war in August 1914, writer Vera
Brittain (1893–1970) wrote in her journal: "Eight
German Zeppelins, the existence of which no
one suspected, are said to be intending to sail
over England, dropping dynamite on our ports &
probably on our rich cities like London. Truly we of
this generation are born to a youth very different
from anything we ever supposed or imagined for
ourselves. Trouble & disasters are menacing us the
nature of which we cannot even guess at."

THE ZEPPELIN RAIDS: THE VOW OF VENGEANCE
Drawn for The Daily Chronicle by Frank Brangwyn ARA

'DAILY CHRONICLE' READERS ARE
COVERED AGAINST THE RISKS OF
BOMBARDMENT BY ZEPPELIN OR
AEROPLANE

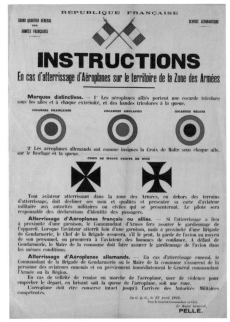

British Official Photo / *New York Journal-American*

British pilots preparing for a raid into enemy territory, June 26, 1918

GELATIN SILVER PRINT

>>> TOP RIGHT

Christina Broom

(British, 1862–1939)

Hand grenades, 1914

GELATIN SILVER PRINT

"Instructions about What to Do If an Airplane Lands in the Territory of the Allied Armies"

April 22, 1916

LITHOGRAPH

Early in the war Allied forces dominated the skies. At the opening of the Battle of the Somme in July 1916, Allied aircraft outnumbered those of the Central powers three to one. In September of that year, however, Germany introduced the new, sleek, and sturdy Albatros D1, which turned German air fighters into aces. The German Air Corps's aerial dominance encouraged star pilot Oswald Boelcke, mentor of the "Red Baron," to draw up a set of guidelines for aerial combat that are still followed by German fighters: "[S]eek the advantage before attacking, attack from the rear and, if possible, with the sun at one's back." This guideline led to an Allied dictum that lasted through both world wars: "Avoid the Hun in the sun."

In the photograph, British Royal Air Force pilots are marking off known enemy positions prior to a dangerous reconnaissance mission across No Man's Land.

In the trenches of the Western Front, the hand grenade (from the French for "pomegranate") quickly replaced the bayonet as one of the most crucial weapons carried by infantry soldiers. Prior to the war, Germany led the combatant nations in production of grenades. By August 1914 the Germans had 70,000 in reserve. The British had produced far fewer of their Mark 1 grenade, which often detonated arbitrarily and was unpopular with Tommy soldiers, who preferred to make "jam tins"—homemade grenades constructed by putting dynamite and metal shards in a jam tin and throwing it into an enemy trench. Their innovation encouraged Britain to develop the Mills bomb, the first modern fragmentation hand grenade to scatter shrapnel as it detonated. By mid-1915 Britain was producing approximately 250,000 Mills bombs a week. Meanwhile, Germany developed bombs specifically designed to release chlorine gas when detonated.

This French army poster familiarized civilians with the various markings on war aircraft. It also outlined the procedures to follow if a French or Allied plane landed outside the designated runway area: keep it safe and notify the nearest garrison. In case of a German plane, however, the population was urged to prevent the pilot from taking off again by "breaking the tail, or a wheel."

Journalists

>>>

Wachtfeuer
(Berlin: Zirkel-Verlag, 1914)

Wachtfeuer (*Watchfire*) was a weekly propaganda magazine published in Berlin between 1914 and 1923. The dramatic cover of this early edition of the magazine features a lone German soldier in a traditional *pickelhaube*, an imposing spiked hat popularized by the Bavarian army in the early nineteenth century. In 1915 the German army replaced the *pickelhaube*, which was easily seen above the parapet of trenches and made infantrymen easy targets for snipers, with a more rounded and sensible steel helmet.

Letter from Winston Churchill to John Fisher
September 16, 1916

During the war the British War Office enjoyed close relationships with many of the most powerful newspaper magnates in the country. Newspaper editor J. L. Garvin, for example, was a confidant of Prime Minister David Lloyd George and Winston Churchill, First Lord of the Admiralty. Garvin's Sunday paper, the *Observer*, became a key propaganda source for the War Office. In this letter from Churchill to navy official John Fisher, a close friend of Garvin's, Churchill lists topics to be promoted in the editorial pages of the *Observer*. Number five on Churchill's list is "ME!"

Ernest Smith's passport
1915–1917

British journalist Ernest Smith traveled throughout Europe during the war, reporting on such events as the Battle of the Somme and the Greek and Russian revolutions. His wartime passports bear the stamps of nearly a dozen nations, and his press badges gave him access to key political figures and combat zones near the Western Front. In his autobiography, *Fields of Adventure* (1923), Smith shocked readers by presenting an insider account of Kaiser Wilhelm II's abdication on November 9, 1918. Smith revealed that though Wilhelm II had not wanted to give up power, he was persuaded to do so after Hindenburg exaggerated reports that civil war had broken out in Germany, threatening the supply line to German troops on the front.

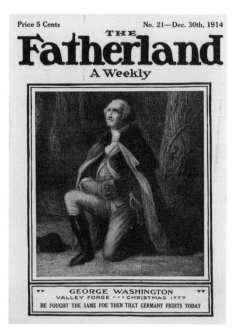

Price 5 Cents   No. 21—Dec. 30th, 1914

THE Fatherland
A Weekly

GEORGE WASHINGTON
VALLEY FORGE ••• CHRISTMAS 1777
HE FOUGHT THE SAME FOE THEN THAT GERMANY FIGHTS TODAY

The Fatherland: A Weekly
December 30, 1914

The poet George Sylvester Viereck (1884–1962) was born in Munich, Germany, and came to the United States with his family in 1896 at the age of 11. His poetry was of a sensual nature and enjoyed popular appeal until 1914. Today he is mostly remembered as an extreme Germanophile who went to prison as a paid propagandist for Nazi Germany during World War II. At the outbreak of the First World War in Europe, however, he began publishing *The Fatherland*, a pro-German journal that reached a circulation of 100,000. The object of the journal was to ensure American neutrality in the war and to help German Americans, or "hyphenated Americans" as he referred to them, counteract anti-German sentiment. This became increasingly hard to do after the sinking of the *Lusitania* in 1915 and impossible after the U.S. entry into war. In February 1917 the journal's name was changed to *New World* and then to *Viereck's The American Weekly*. Viereck was expelled from the Authors' League of America for his political beliefs, and in 1918 he admitted receiving $100,000 from German interests during a government investigation of his propaganda activities.

Letter from Henry Major Tomlinson to his wife, Florence
September 4, 1914

H. M. Tomlinson (1873–1958) began the war as a journalist for the London *Daily News* and later served as an official war correspondent for the British army. He spent much of the war near the French and Belgian front lines. In this letter to his wife, Tomlinson describes a close brush with German troops while fleeing Belgium by train and expresses his frustration over the censorship enforced by British officials, whom he accuses of playing favorites. He writes, "There is a lot I could tell you, old lady, but this letter will probably be opened and read by an official. . . . I have played the game fairly with the authorities; but they have not played it fairly with some of us. They allow the *Times* and the *Daily Mail* to do things and say things which some of us, for a good many reasons, would never think of asking permission to do."

Photographers

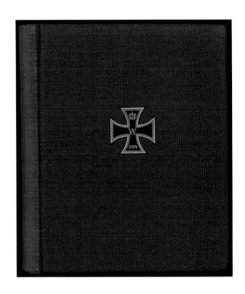

>>>

An album of German postcards,
taken from original photos by
A. Grohs, A. Kühlewindt, R. Sennecke,
M. Obergassner, and others
(Berlin: chiefly published by Gustav Liersch, 1914)

Cheap, mass-produced, and easy to pass by the
censor, the picture postcard became an item used
for propaganda by all the nations at war during
1914–1918. This album contains cards that reproduce
pictures taken by official German war photographers.
From Kaiser and cavalry to artillery and infantry, the
images emphasize the strength and numbers of the
Central powers.

New York Journal-American
U.S. Signal Corps officer with a camera, ca. 1917
GELATIN SILVER PRINT

In World War I the newly established Photographic Section of the American Signal Corps was responsible for ground and combat photographs, as well as the aerial photographs, mapping, and reconnaissance produced by affixing cameras to airplanes or balloons. The U.S. Army controlled all combat photography, and civilian photographers were not allowed to operate close to the front lines. By the end of the war, Signal Corps photographers had taken nearly 30,000 still pictures, most of which were developed in mobile darkrooms behind the lines. The army used these photographs for training, propaganda, and documentation purposes. Army censors maintained a strict policy against publishing any pictures of dead U.S. soldiers. The most graphic photographs collected by the Signal Corps were not released to the general public until nearly a decade after the war's end.

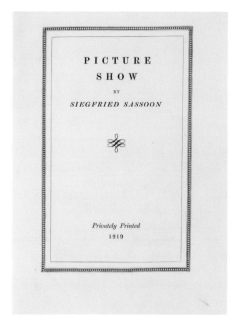

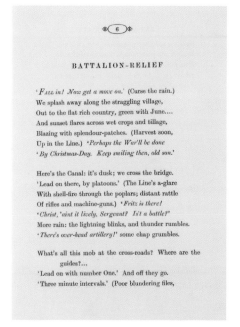

Annotated and extra-illustrated copy of Siegfried Sassoon's *Picture Show*
1919

As the war drew to a close, British poet Siegfried Sassoon (1886–1967) collected his elegies and antiwar verse together in the volume *Picture Show*. In his personal copy of the book, Sassoon pasted in multiple government-censored photographs of dead soldiers on the battlefields of the Western Front. These images were strictly forbidden from publication during the war.

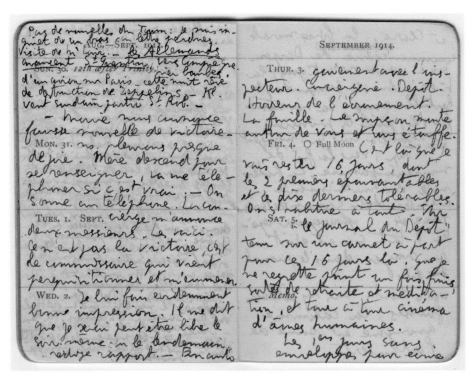

Diary entry of Henri-Pierre Roché
August 30–September 5, 1914

The French writer and flâneur Henri-Pierre Roché (1879–1959) was declared unfit for combat because of problems with his knees. Because of his large number of "foreign friends," including the German writer Franz Hessel (1880–1941), and "copious international correspondence," an anonymous detractor denounced Roché to the authorities. Accused of espionage, he spent 16 days in the Conciergerie prison, where aristocrats were guillotined during the French Revolution. Roché wrote of his imprisonment: "[T]he first two [days] were appalling, and the last ten were tolerable. One can get used to anything." Roché's various cell mates included a debt collector, a waiter, an American millionaire, a pimp, a juvenile delinquent, a dancer, and a gambler, who was also a former professor of Greek.

Unidentified photographer
Henri-Pierre Roché, 1914
GELATIN SILVER PRINT

10   *Deux semaines à la Conciergerie*

La cellule.

A travers un corridor et une grande cour couverte, je suis mené dans une cellule à trois lits, deux portes et deux fenêtres haut placées. Avant d'entrer, je remarque qu'il y a encore deux étages de cellules au-dessus de ma tête.

La porte et les verrous claquent avec une force que je ne croyais possible que dans les romans.

Seul. Je m'assieds sur le lit le plus près de la porte, pour sortir vite, dès qu'on m'appellera.

Jusqu'ici, tout cela m'a intéressé. Même si je reste une nuit, ce sera vite passé.

Le jour tombe. Les fenêtres ont des barreaux

Spies

»»

Proclamation announcing Edith Cavell's death sentence and immediate execution for treason
October 12, 1915

British nurse Edith Cavell (1865–1915) was the head of a nursing school, L'École belge d'infirmières diplômées, in Brussels, Belgium. After the Battle of Mons, Edith Cavell and her friends nursed wounded Allied soldiers who had been caught behind the lines in German-occupied Belgium and smuggled them across the border into neutral Holland. On August 5, 1915, Cavell was arrested by the Germans and sent to St. Gilles prison. She was found guilty of treason and sentenced to death. On the evening before her execution, she spoke with Reverend Horace Stirling Townsend Gahan, the English chaplain of Christ Church, telling him, "This I would say, standing as I do in view of God and Eternity, I realize that patriotism is not enough. I must have no hatred or bitterness towards anyone." She was executed the next morning along with Philippe Baucq, an architect, whose last words were "Vive la Belgique!"

   Germans produced this poster in occupied Belgium as a warning to the population: "The Governor-General of Brussels Publicizes These Facts So That They May Serve as a Warning."

‹‹‹ FACING PAGE, BOTTOM RIGHT

Henri-Pierre Roché's *Deux semaines à la Conciergerie pendant la bataille de la Marne*
(Paris: Attinger Frères, 1916)
Author's inscribed copy to critic Émile Vuillermoz

Roché looked back with some humor on his imprisonment. He published an account that was first serialized in the Parisian journal *Le Temps* and subsequently published as a monograph with illustrations by Robert Bonfils (1886–1972). Roché (1879–1959) eventually was made secretary to General Gabriel Malleterre (1858–1923), Governor General of the Invalides, who had lost a leg in battle during the first weeks of the war.

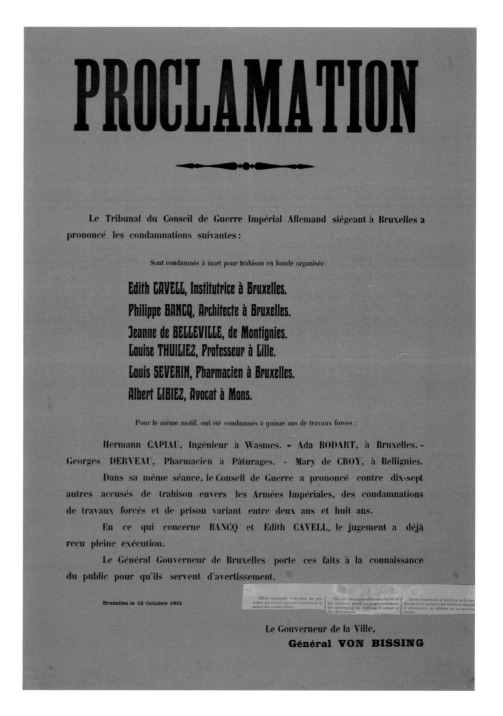

*Sir Mansfield Cumming
Chief of Secret Service
1918*

4th May. 1918

WHITEHALL COURT,
S.W.1.

My dear Compton Mackenzie,

Many thanks for your letter and for the honour you propose to confer on me by dedicating to me one of your books. I should indeed be very gratified and hope it will be up to your usual form. You told me once that all chorus girls liked your books and I am afraid I must plead guilty to belonging to the same category - I hope it doesn't show any particular evil tendency. All goes well here. We have had a deuce of a fight over the job (which every one seems to think that they are specially cut out for). In spite of all attacks from folks in high places, I am still here and going strong. Far from closing down - as we thought we should have to do after the war - we are actually expanding, and we have any amount of work to do in the immediate future. Many of our staff have gone I am sorry to say, but there are still some left. My own plans have been completely upset from not being broad or ambitious enough, and I have now to expand the office and re-organise so as to cover a wider field. This is of course very satisfactory from my point of view and I hope and think that we shall get a good show going before long. I am over head and ears in work and see no prospect of any rest. Good bye, let me know if you change your plans at all. I hope the neuritis is leaving you alone for a spell.

yours ever,

P.T.O.

PS. I think it would be as well to disguise me under the title of "C" or "The Chief" or something similar ?

Letter from Mansfield Cumming to Compton Mackenzie
May 4, 1918

When *Greek Memories* was published in 1932, Mackenzie was accused of violating the Official Secrets Act for revealing that Mansfield Cumming (1859–1923) was the chief of the British Secret Intelligence Service (now MI6), disclosing the names of several other active agents, and divulging details of British intelligence operations. Although many of Mackenzie's revelations were already well known, the book was banned and Mackenzie put on trial. He pled guilty and was fined £100. An expurgated version of the book was published in 1939. In this letter, Mansfield thanks Mackenzie for dedicating his latest book, *Poor Relations*, to him but asks that his identity be kept secret and that he be referred to as "C," his code name, or "Chief." To this day, as a tribute to Mansfield Cumming, the chief of MI6 goes by "C" and adopts his custom of signing papers with green ink.

Unidentified photographer
Lieutenant Compton Mackenzie, ca. 1915
GELATIN SILVER PRINT

At the end of August 1915, after "being a butterfly in the graveyard of Gallipoli," British author Compton Mackenzie (1883–1972), a lieutenant in the Royal Marines, was sent to neutral Greece to be the head of British counterespionage in Athens. Adopting the code name "Z" and dressing in a white suit and hat, while being chauffeured by a Greek soldier wearing the traditional white fustanella, a sort of kilt, Mackenzie did not try to blend in. Yet, as the head of counterespionage, he was extremely successful, and he soon controlled much of the counterintelligence in the Aegean. He moved the counterespionage headquarters to the British School of Archaeology and employed its librarian to help organize the Black List, a catalog of enemy agents and informers. Mackenzie also centralized control of visa applications in the Z Bureau—as his office was known—where the names and details on applications were immediately added to the Black List.

>>> FACING PAGE

Notes on a secret meeting by Major Monreal to Major Samson
ca. 1915

When first posted to Athens, Compton Mackenzie worked under Major Monreal (a.k.a. "M," "Liebig," and "L"), who was head of British counterespionage in Athens. Monreal sent notes about a meeting with possible German spies to Major Samson (a.k.a. "R" and "V"), his superior and head of intelligence in Athens. Monreal was quickly posted to Malta after he started plotting unauthorized assassinations of enemy agents.

I was in my hiding-place before
the meeting started but when I
saw pistols on the table I dare not
+ move round + my
cold preventing me from
hearing better. As far I could
gather the following were present:
1) Baron de Grancy
2) a youngster called Papadopoulos
(a relation of Papadopoulos-Laurin)
3) a fellow called Athanassion or
something of the kind who is
concerned with bomb-making
Piraeus.
4) a man called Erzberger whom I could not see
A man called **Braun**
who seems to be an interpreter
in Athens, + who has just returned

from Salonica.
a Greek full colonel; I could
see the gilt on his cap + the
rattling of his sword. — Particulars of
Grancy began by saying
that Schenk was suffering from
the same complaint as the King
that he had been removed to
the second floor + that a doctor
was coming from Germany.
After this, the following statements
were uttered by various people:
the conversation
throughout was in French. —
Grancy said something about
having no money + that Baron
Schenk unable to pay. — the
Greek Colonel said as Schenk

was a share-holder of Krupps he
ought to pay out of his own
pocket. — **Braun** (*) said the
landing at Salonika was all
"balls." there were only 3000 men
Somebody said a wire had
just been received from Assima-
copoulo that the " U " 99.
had been taken by the Allies. —
Then followed a discussion as to
whether it had been taken by the
English, French or Italian + I
caught the names, Kythera, Argos
+ Kriti. It appears the submarine
has not been sunk but captured
Grancy told someone to find
a house for the 3 men of Conspl.
Grancy at the end of the

performance gave a 1000
franc note to the caretaker

Marica's name propped up
repeatedly. This is the Marica
for whom Georghi your porter
was caught carrying a letter
to the German centre in
Themistokli's Street.

Morgan's name
repeatedly uttered in
connection with Cavalla +
Consple

> "Keep quiet! Be careful! Enemy ears are listening!"
> ca. 1915

Frederic Dorr Steele
(American, 1873–1944)
Illustration of Sherlock Holmes in *Collier's Magazine*, September 22, 1917

In 1917, to help the war effort, Arthur Conan Doyle (1859–1930) brought his fictional detective Sherlock Holmes out of retirement. In this short story, published simultaneously in *Strand Magazine* and *Collier's*, Holmes sabotages the German war effort by passing on false information and captures German spy Von Bork on the eve of the war. In this adventure, Holmes is disguised as an Irish American "with clear-cut features and a small goatee beard which gave him a general resemblance to the caricatures of Uncle Sam."

At the end of *His Last Bow*, Sherlock Holmes declares to Dr. Watson, "Good old Watson! You are the one fixed point in a changing age. There's an east wind coming all the same, such a wind as never blew on England yet. It will be cold and bitter, Watson, and a good many of us may wither before its blast. But it's God's own wind none the less, and a cleaner, better, stronger land will lie in the sunshine when the storm has cleared."

Doyle served as a military correspondent during the war. His son Kingsley (1892–1918) was wounded in the Battle of the Somme in 1916 and died during the influenza epidemic in 1918.

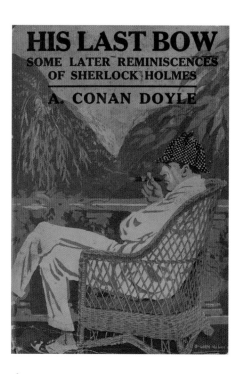

> Arthur Conan Doyle's *His Last Bow*
> (New York: G. H. Doran, ca. 1917)

Ambulance Drivers and Medics

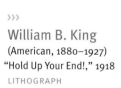

William B. King
(American, 1880–1927)
"Hold Up Your End!," 1918
LITHOGRAPH

The American Red Cross, established in 1881, experienced phenomenal growth during the First World War. Between 1914 and 1918 American Red Cross membership jumped from 17,000 to more than 20 million members. Its bold advertising and publicity campaigns encouraged the American public to donate more than $400 million to Red Cross programs that staffed Allied hospitals in France, provided ambulance drivers, and gave medical care to refugees. The Red Cross recruited 20,000 registered nurses to serve the military during the war, and many of them continued to work with the Red Cross during the postwar influenza pandemic that killed an estimated 20–40 million people worldwide.

This poster was created for the American Red Cross's second and highly successful war-fund drive in 1918.

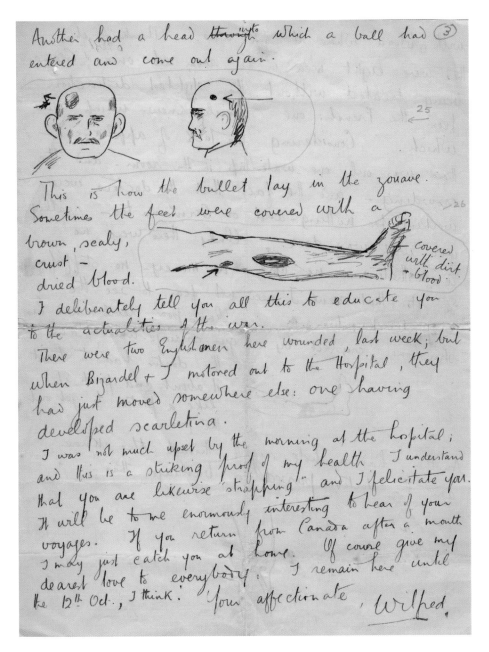

Another had a head through into which a ball had ③ entered and come out again.

This is how the bullet lay in the zouave. Sometimes the feet were covered with a brown, scaly, crust — dried blood.

covered with dirt + blood

I deliberately tell you all this to educate you to the actualities of the war.

There were two Englishmen here wounded, last week; but when Bizardel & I motored out to the Hospital, they had just moved somewhere else: one having developed scarletina.

I was not much upset by the morning at the hospital; and this is a striking proof of my health. I understand that you are likewise 'strapping' and I felicitate you. It will be to me enormously interesting to hear of your voyages. If you return from Canada after a month I may just catch you at home. Of course give my dearest love to everybody. I remain here until the 12th Oct., I think. Your affectionate, Wilfred.

‹‹‹

Letter from Wilfred Owen to his brother Harold
September 23, 1914

At the outbreak of war, British poet Wilfred Owen (1893–1918) was working as an English tutor in the city of Bordeaux, a short distance from the Western Front. One month after hostilities began, Owen visited one of the town's hastily built army hospitals. In this letter to his younger brother Harold, he drew pictures of the gruesome bullet wounds he saw while touring the hospital, warning, "I deliberately tell you all this to educate you to the actualities of the war." Wilfred Owen joined the British armed services in 1915; Harold joined the following year.

››› FACING PAGE, TOP

International News Photo / *New York Journal-American*
Wounded soldiers awaiting transport, not dated
GELATIN SILVER PRINT

Minor and mortal injuries were treated immediately on the Western Front, but soldiers who received injuries such as broken limbs or minor bullet wounds were sent home indefinitely. These wounds were known among the British as a "Blighty one" (the slang term "Blighty," meaning England, derived from colonial soldiers' mispronunciation of the Hindi word for "foreign"). A soldier with one of these wounds could be sent into homeland domestic service, which many soldiers found preferable to the danger of the trenches. The desirability of a "Blighty one" was so high that the army enforced court-martial and death sentences for soldiers found guilty of self-inflicted wounds.

>>>

New York Journal-American
Disabled veterans returning home from the Western Front, ca. 1918
GELATIN SILVER PRINT

The severely wounded American Expeditionary Force "doughboys" in this photograph represent the nearly 20 million nonfatal casualties of the First World War. The use of industrialized weapons such as the machine gun and trench mortar made shrapnel wounds and amputations commonplace and made doctors—especially surgeons—among the most valued members of the armed services. By 1918 more than half of Britain's doctors were in service with the armed forces. By decree they were not allowed near the front lines, where their lives would be jeopardized. The majority of doctors treated soldiers in "casualty clearing stations," where they were forced to make triage decisions concerning whether a soldier's wounds were too severe to be treated.

Edward Penfield
(American, 1866–1925)
"Yes Sir—I Am Here!," ca. 1918
LITHOGRAPH

The shortage of trained medical personnel impelled American and British forces to recruit women as ambulance drivers. Female ambulance drivers worked long hours transporting troops on bad roads, were responsible for the maintenance of their automobiles, and administered basic first aid before the troops reached field hospitals behind the lines. In this Motor Corps of America recruitment poster, the female ambulance driver wears an androgynous uniform consisting of an army tunic, military cap, tie, and skirt.

Unidentified photographer
Ernest Hemingway in uniform, ca. 1918
GELATIN SILVER PRINT

This photograph, probably taken outside the Ospedale Maggiore War Hospital in Milan, shows a convalescing Hemingway leaning on a cane and wearing his Red Cross Ambulance Corps uniform. When Hemingway returned from Italy to his hometown, the Chicago suburb of Oak Park, Illinois, he gave a series of speeches about his war experience to area high schools, churches, and clubs, all while wearing his uniform. A local paper reported that during his lecture at Oak Park High School, Hemingway carried a captured Austrian revolver and gas mask and held up his punctured, bloodstained trousers as proof of his war stories.

Ultimately unable to readjust to postwar civilian life, Hemingway left the United States for Paris in 1922, where he would write his celebrated Lost Generation novel *The Sun Also Rises* (1926).

›››

Unidentified photographer
Gertrude Stein and Alice B. Toklas in front of Joffre's birthplace, 1917
PHOTOGRAPHIC POSTCARD

Expatriate American author Gertrude Stein (1874–1946) and her companion Alice B. Toklas (1877–1967) were living in Mallorca, Spain, when the Battle of Verdun compelled them to return home to Paris. They ordered a Ford van, which they nicknamed "Auntie" "after Gertrude Stein's aunt Pauline who always behaved admirably in emergencies and behaved fairly well most times if she was properly flattered," and went to work for the American Fund for French Wounded. They were delivering hospital supplies to Rivesaltes when they were photographed outside Maréchal Joffre's birthplace. The photograph was made into postcards, which were sold to raise money for the American Fund.

Birth Place of Marechal JOFFRE at Rivesaltes april 1917

Revolutionaries

›››

Eric Kennington's portrait of
T. E. Lawrence from the first edition
of Lawrence's *Seven Pillars of
Wisdom*
(London: Printed by M. Pike with the assistance
of H. J. Hodgson, 1926)

T. E. Lawrence, or "Lawrence of Arabia," was one of
the most famous figures to emerge from the First
World War. Lawrence's chronicle of his war experiences is accompanied by maps, woodcuts, and
reproductions of paintings and drawings by such
well-known artists as Eric Kennington, Augustus
John, and Paul Nash. Originally, Lawrence intended
to print only a few copies of the book to give as
gifts to friends and family but, after much coaxing,
agreed reluctantly to make it available to the public.
Although *Seven Pillars of Wisdom* was a popular
success and made Lawrence of Arabia a national
hero, it also nearly bankrupted Lawrence; he had
privately printed only 200 copies and sold them at a
fraction of the production cost. To pay off his debts,
Lawrence agreed to the commercial publication of
an inexpensive abridged version of his autobiography, *Revolt in the Desert* (1927). Lawrence's publisher sold 150,000 copies within four months.

Eric Kennington
(British, 1888–1960)
Emir Abdullah, 1920
CHARCOAL ON PAPER
With permission from the family of the artist

For the 1926 edition of *Seven Pillars of Wisdom*, Kennington created this portrait of Emir Abdullah (1882–1951), son of King Hussein, ruler of the Arab tribes in the years leading up to the First World War. In 1914 Abdullah convinced his father that the outbreak of war in Europe provided the perfect opportunity to stage an uprising against Turkish rule in the Middle East.

Abdullah appealed to Britain as a mutual enemy of the Ottoman Empire, hoping that the Allied powers would provide support to his father's ill-equipped armies. He secretly met with Lord Kitchener, British Secretary of State for War, who provided weapons for the Husseins' guerrilla campaign in Mesopotamia and the Sinai Peninsula. The British high command also sent the young officer T. E. Lawrence, who fought alongside Abdullah and Abdullah's brother Faisal, later King of Iraq, during the 1916–1918 campaigns in Aqaba and Damascus. After the defeat of Turkish rule, Lawrence, working as an aide to Winston Churchill, helped Abdullah and Faisal establish independent Arab states in the Middle East. In his memoir Abdullah wrote that though he resented Western influence among the Arab tribes, Lawrence "was regarded as the moving spirit in the Revolt."

‹‹‹

George Nathaniel Nash
(British, 1888–?)
Parade in Saint Petersburg after the
February Revolution, ca. 1917
GELATIN SILVER PRINT

In these photographs taken by British Lieutenant
George Nathaniel Nash, stationed as an artillery
officer and translator in Russia from 1917 to 1919
and witness to the February and October Revolutions, the banners read "Down with the 10 Capitalist
Ministers," "Proletariat of the Country Unite!," and
"Long Live Socialism!"

››› FACING PAGE, LEFT

Ilya Yefimovich Repin
(Russian, 1844–1930)
Portrait of Alexsandr Fyodorovich Kerensky, 1917
OIL ON BOARD

Alexsandr Fyodorovich Kerensky (1881–1970) was
named Minister of Justice in the Provisional Government formed after the Russian Revolution. He was
a popular lawyer and the only Socialist in the new
government. Although Trotsky would characterize
him as someone who "hung around the Revolution,"
Kerensky's fiery and emotional speeches created a
movement that some described as a cult following.
Made Minister of War and then Prime Minister of the
Provisional Government, Kerensky was ridiculed for
emulating Napoleon by taking up residence in the
Czar's quarters, cuffing his hand inside the breast of
his uniform, and wearing a fabricated military uniform even though he was never in service.

›››

Boris Mikhailovich Kustodiev
(Russian, 1878–1927)
"Заемъ Свободы / Liberty Loan," ca. 1917
LITHOGRAPH

In 1917 Russia was fighting two wars: one against
the Central powers and the other against its own
government. After the abdication of Czar Nicholas
II following the February Revolution, a provisional
government took over. On the Eastern Front, Russian
troops were in desperate need of supplies. To raise
money for the war effort, the Provisional Government began issuing "Liberty Loans" in March 1917.
A series of contests were held for the best artwork
advertising the loans. Winning images were displayed in newspapers, on postcards, and on posters such as this one. The campaign failed to raise
money or morale. Citizens were distrustful of the
loans and reluctant to support the "war until victory"
stance of the Provisional Government.

Axel Malmström
(Swedish, 1872–1945)
Lenin arrives in Stockholm en route to Russia, 1917
GELATIN SILVER PRINT

Following the February Revolution, Germany aided Vladimir Ilyich Lenin (1870–1924) in his return from exile in Geneva, Switzerland. The Germans slipped him across Europe's borders on a "sealed" train on April 3, 1917. British officer George Nathaniel Nash noted in his diary about Lenin's return, "[T]his is bad as he is one of the 'down with the war' type[s]."

94

Sir Roger Casement:- "Officially I am Sir Roger Casement."

~~The A.C.C. pointed out to him that there might be some~~ ~~people impersonating Casement, and the reply made with~~ ~~some bitterness was~~ THE. A.C.C. "There may be people impersonating Sir Roger Casement"

Sir Roger Casement. ⎰ "I don't think there are many people who would care to impersonate me."

The A.C.C.:- "Of course you know your own position perfectly, because you are not bound to answer any question put to you, and any reply you make will be used in evidence against you."

Sir Roger Casement:- "May I ask what you charge me with?"

The A.C.C.:- "You are not charged."

Sir Roger Casement:- "I was charged on arrest in Kerry by the constable who arrested me."

The A.C.C.:- "What did he say to you when he charged you?"

Sir Roger Casement. "With aiding to land arms on the coast of Kerry."

The A.C.C.:- "You made no reply to that."

Sir Roger Casement:- "I said I should ask for legal advice."

The A.C.C.:- "You are not charged at present but it is certain that you will be."

Casement was then shown the railway sleeping car ticket No 0113 from Berlin to Wilhelmshaven available for the night of the 11-12th of April, which was found in the pocket of one of three coats at McKenna's fort.

"Is that your property?" he was asked.

Montgomery Hyde's transcript of Roger Casement's interrogation at Scotland Yard
1916

Roger Casement (1864–1916) was an Irish revolutionary who joined the Irish Volunteers in 1914 after retiring from his post as a British consul. Casement and fellow revolutionary Joseph Plunkett secured German guns, ammunition, and troops for the planned Easter Rising, but the British intercepted the disguised German ship carrying 20,000 rifles and ammunition on April 20, 1916. Casement was captured and arrested the next day off the coast of Kerry shortly after disembarking from a German submarine. Casement was tried for treason, sabotage, and espionage against the Crown. He freely admitted to conspiring with the Germans in the name of Irish independence but refused to recognize the validity of his trial. He was an Irishman in a foreign court, and if he were to be tried at all, he insisted it should be "in Ireland, before an Irish court, and by an Irish jury." Casement was found guilty on all counts, sentenced to death, and executed in London on August 3, 1916.

Pacifists

>>>

Letter from George Bernard Shaw to Austin Harrison
November 24, 1914

Irish playwright George Bernard Shaw (1856–1950)
published his antiwar pamphlet *Common Sense
about the War* just weeks after armed conflict broke
out in Europe. Some 75,000 copies were sold in
six weeks. Subsequently, Shaw was accused of
treasonous pro-German sympathies (he quipped
that angry readers thought of him as a "son of a
bitsch"). In a letter to Austin Harrison, editor of the
English Review, Shaw explains that he wishes for a
shift in human beings' relationship to violence: "It
is utter nonsense to say that if you keep guns they
will go off: people can wear boots without kicking
their wives."

AYOT ST LAWRENCE, WELWYN, HERTS.
STATION: WHEATHAMPSTEAD, G.N.R.2¼ MILES.
TELEGRAMS: BERNARD SHAW, CODICOTE.

AA-6   IO ADELPHI TERRACE.W.C.

24th november 1914.

Dear Austin Harrison

Where does the necessity for disarmament come in ? We are teaching
all the savages on earth to use modern weapons and dig themselves in and
all the rest of it. How can we sanely leave civilization defenceless
in such a den of wild beasts? What we can do is to make a combination
against war, as such -- an armed and violent combination limited to the
countries west of the Vistula as a matter of simple manageability and
contiguity. It is utter nonsense to say that if you keep guns they will
go off : people can wear boots without kicking their wives. I dont suppose anything like one per cent of the guns supplied to soldiers have
ever been fired at a human target.

I have dealt with the point ; but the confounded thing is so long
that nobody reads it through.

yours ever
G. Bernard Shaw.

The poem will show
you what I feel like. And it is the truth.

TELEGRAMS: "WARSPITAL SLATEFORD."
TELEPHONE: CENTRAL 8250.

CRAIGLOCKHART WAR HOSPITAL,

SLATEFORD,

MIDLOTHIAN.

Wednesday

My dear Ottoline

Your letter reached me just as I was moving my belongings
into the 'garret' which I have at length secured & am
now free from theosophy & conversation, though somewhat
chilly.   As you say the war situation looks more
hopeless than ever, & the bolstering speeches only
make it seem worse.   I am afraid I cannot do
anything 'outrageous'. They would only say I had a
relapse & put me in a padded room. I am
at present faced with the prospect of remaining
here for an indefinite period & you can imagine
how what that affects me.   Apparently nothing that
I can do will make them take me seriously (& of
course it is the obvious course for them to
adopt).   I have told Rivers that I will not
withdraw anything that I have said or written, & that
my views are the same — but that I will go back
to France if the W.O. will give me a guarantee that
they really will send me there.   I haven't the
least idea what they will do. But I hope you

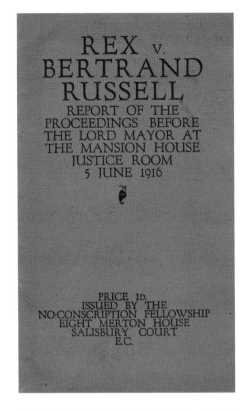

REX v. BERTRAND RUSSELL

REPORT OF THE
PROCEEDINGS BEFORE
THE LORD MAYOR AT
THE MANSION HOUSE
JUSTICE ROOM
5 JUNE 1916

PRICE 1D.
ISSUED BY THE
NO·CONSCRIPTION FELLOWSHIP
EIGHT MERTON HOUSE
SALISBURY COURT
E.C.

Letter from Siegfried Sassoon to Ottoline Morrell, written from Craiglockhart War Hospital

1917

© Siegfried Sassoon by kind permission of the Estate of George Sassoon

Lady Ottoline Morrell (1873–1938) provided a safe haven for pacifists and conscientious objectors at her large country estate, Garsington Manor. Along with her lover, philosopher Bertrand Russell, Morrell supported a British peace treaty with Germany. During the war, politicians and intellectuals began referring to a "Garsington Peace Movement" promoted by Morrell and such artists as D. H. Lawrence, Dora Carrington, Augustus John, Clive Bell, and Lytton Strachey.

Siegfried Sassoon convalesced at Garsington after being wounded in battle on the Western Front in 1917. While there, Sassoon drafted his famous "Finished with the War: A Soldier's Declaration," in which he refused to return to active duty because he believed that the war was being disastrously prolonged.

When in July 1917 Sassoon's declaration was read in the British Parliament and widely printed, the British army announced that the army captain was suffering from shell shock and sent him to Craiglockhart War Hospital, where he wrote Morrell: "I am afraid I can't do anything 'outrageous.' They would only say I had a relapse and put me in a padded room."

Rex v. Bertrand Russell

(London: No-Conscription Fellowship, 1916)

Cambridge philosophy professor Bertrand Russell (1872–1970) was one of the most vocal British antiwar activists. In 1916 Russell wrote a pamphlet in support of Ernest Everett, a conscientious objector who had been imprisoned for his refusal to serve in the military. Russell was tried under the Defense of the Realm Act and fined for hampering recruiting. This booklet, published by the No-Conscription Fellowship, of which Russell was chairman, documented Russell's rebuttals to the government's indictment. Two years later, Russell was once again arrested for spreading antiwar literature and served six months in prison.

Unidentified photographer
E. E. Cummings in uniform, 1918
GELATIN SILVER PRINT

Letter from Rebecca Cummings to E. E. Cummings
November 1917

American poet E. E. Cummings (1894–1962) avoided the American army by volunteering for the Norton-Harjes Ambulance Service in France. A committed pacifist, he suffered a series of misadventures during his service. Cummings tried to exasperate censors by hinting at his location and composing caricatures of his superiors. But when Cummings wrote about his reluctance to kill Germans, he was arrested and sent to a prisoner-of-war camp. Cummings's 1922 memoir, *The Enormous Room*, tells of his incarceration.

During his internment, E. E. Cummings's letters to his family were withheld and his identity confused with that of another soldier. His family received an erroneous cable that Cummings had been lost at sea when the ship *Antilles* was torpedoed by a German submarine.

In this letter, Cummings's mother expresses her joy and relief after the State Department cabled the family to clarify that it had been "H. H. Cummings" rather than E. E. Cummings who had been lost on the sunken ship. Cummings was released from the prisoner-of-war camp in December 1917.

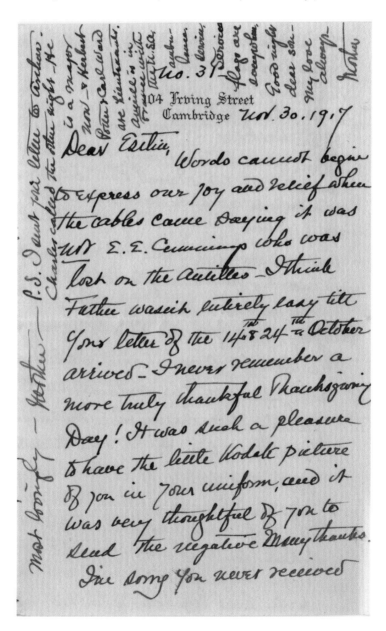

Politicians

››

New York Journal-American

**American Secretary of War Newton Baker pulling
the first draft number, July 20, 1917**

GELATIN SILVER PRINT

The U.S. Selective Service Act of 1917 allowed
Woodrow Wilson's administration to raise an army
through conscription. Though Wilson had planned
to enlarge the U.S. Army with an aggressive recruitment campaign, volunteers were not as forthcoming
as he had hoped. Wilson accepted the advice of
Secretary of War Newton Baker, who implemented
a nationwide draft. Baker also established the Committee for Public Information, the American government's first official propaganda organization. This
committee, run by politicians and ex–newspaper
magnates, used a variety of media to influence public opinion and popularize American war aims.

‹‹‹

Heinrich Hoffman, *Hitler Was My Friend* (London: Burke Publishing, 1955)
Adolf Hitler (standing far left) with fellow soldiers, ca. 1917
GELATIN SILVER PRINT

During the First World War, future Nazi leader Adolf Hitler served as a dispatch runner for a Bavarian infantry unit, earning the rank of corporal. He was severely wounded during the Battle of the Somme and was decorated with the Iron Cross. In his autobiography, *Mein Kampf*, Hitler claimed that his experiences as a soldier in the war, as well as his anger over the war reparations exacted from Germany in the Treaty of Versailles, deeply influenced his postwar politics. Hitler considered his service as a German infantryman "the greatest and most unforgettable time of [his] earthly existence" and found that after the war "the rage of the international exploiters of our people in Versailles was directed primarily against the old German army." Throughout the 1920s Hitler traveled throughout Germany delivering speeches titled "The True Causes of the World War" and "The Peace Treaties of Brest-Litovsk and Versailles." They were enormously popular with audiences and contributed to the rise to power of the National Socialist German Workers'—later Nazi—Party.

‹‹‹

Unidentified Photographer
Woodrow Wilson saluting American Expeditionary Force troops, ca. 1917
GELATIN SILVER PRINT

On April 2, 1917, President Woodrow Wilson solemnly urged Congress to put aside neutrality and join the Allied war effort in Europe. Wilson specifically cited the submarine attacks against American civilian ships as cause for declaring war against Germany:

> I am not now thinking of the loss of property involved, immense and serious as that is, but only of the wanton and wholesale destruction of the lives of non-combatants, men, women, and children, engaged in pursuits which have always, even in the darkest periods of modern history, been deemed innocent and legitimate. Property can be paid for; the lives of peaceful and innocent people cannot be. The present German submarine warfare against commerce is a warfare against mankind.

The American declaration of war against Germany was signed four days after Wilson's speech.

Unidentified photographer
Winston Churchill watching the military parade of the British 47th Division after the liberation of Lille
October 28, 1918
GELATIN SILVER PRINT

At the end of the war, 44-year-old Winston Churchill (1874–1965), who had nearly wrecked his political career after planning the disastrous 1915 British campaign in the Dardanelles, served as Prime Minister David Lloyd George's Minister of Munitions.

In this photograph, taken just a few weeks before Armistice, Churchill pensively watches the military parade of Allied forces after the liberation of the French city of Lille. Standing in front and to the left of Churchill is Bernard Montgomery, who would later lead the British army during World War II. In 1944 Prime Minister Churchill would assign "Monty" to plan and execute Operation Overlord, the D-Day invasion of Normandy. After the success of Operation Overlord, Churchill made Montgomery Field Marshal of the British army. On May 4, 1945, Montgomery would accept the surrender of the Germans, effectively ending World War II in Europe.

Though the combined efforts of the two men helped draw World War II to an Allied victory, they sustained a famously antagonistic relationship. In his memoir, *Ambrosia and Small Beer* (1965), Edward Marsh, Churchill's personal secretary (standing behind Churchill, wearing a bowler hat), wrote that Churchill famously claimed that Montgomery was "in defeat, unbeatable; in victory, unbearable."

Children

Urquhart Wilcox
(American, 1874–1941)
"'We'll Help You to Win the War, Dad,' with
War Savings Stamps," ca. 1917
LITHOGRAPH

The Boy Scouts of America were leading fund-raisers
for the war effort in the United States. In 1917–1918
the Boy Scouts sold more than $350 million in war
bonds and more than $100 million in war savings
stamps. They also collected fruit pits that were
ground into charcoal to be used in gas masks and
inventoried trees that could be used for the production of airplane propellers.

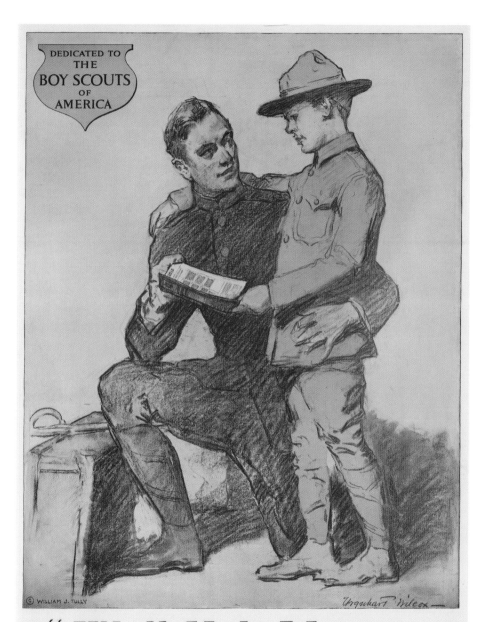

From Evelyn Waugh's childhood diary. © 2013 by Evelyn Waugh, used by permission of The Wylie Agency LLC

<<<

Evelyn Waugh's diaries,
1914–1919

British novelist Evelyn Waugh (1903–1966) was 11 years old when the war broke out. These diaries chronicle his experience of wartime England while he was at Heath Mount preparatory school.

Waugh's mother served as a volunteer army nurse, and Waugh and his father visited London hospitals to perform humorous skits for convalescing soldiers. In the summer of 1915 Waugh served as a messenger for the British War Office, and in 1917 Waugh's older brother Alec enlisted and was sent to France.

One diary depicts one of his schoolmasters, "Mr. Vernon," who enlisted in 1914. Waugh has written, "I feel rather sorry now I used to rag him so." Another illustrates a mock trench built by Waugh and his fellow Boy Scouts. The Scouts charged nearby residents a fee to walk through the makeshift trench, then donated the proceeds to the national war fund.

Waugh was known for his outspoken manner and hatred of hypocrisy. By 1919, when Waugh was 16 years old, he had already developed strong opinions about the way the war should be commemorated. On November 11, 1919, the day of the cease-fire, he wrote:

> At eleven today we had the King's amazing proposition of two minutes silence to commemorate last year. It was really a disgusting idea of artificial nonsense and sentimentality. If people have lost sons and fathers they should think of them whenever the grass is green or Shaftsbury Avenue brightly lighted, not for two minutes on the anniversary of a disgraceful day of national hysteria.

<<<

Letter from Wilfred Owen to Colin Owen
August 23, 1916

British soldier-poet Wilfred Owen (1893–1918) wrote faithfully to his family from the trenches of the Western Front. Owen particularly doted on his younger brother Colin, who was only 14 when war erupted in Europe. Owen desperately hoped that Colin would be saved from the war, writing, "Your tender age is a thing to be valued and gloried in, more than many wounds." Colin, who idolized his brother, joined the Royal Flying Corps in 1917, against Wilfred's wishes. He withdrew from the military after Wilfred Owen was killed in France a week before the cease-fire.

Ze n'ai pas peur des "Boches"!

JOURNÉE DE PARIS

AU PROFIT DES ŒUVRES DE GUERRE DE L'HÔTEL DE VILLE

14 JUILLET 1917

VISÉ N° S.936   EDITEUR IMP. H.CHACHOIN, 108, Rue Folie-Méricourt.

≫

Francisque Poulbot
(French, 1879–1946)
Cartoon
PEN AND INK

⟩⟩⟩

Francisque Poulbot
(French, 1879–1946)
Paris Day, on Behalf of the Hôtel de Ville's War Charities, 14 July 1917

The drawings of Poulbot, who is famous for his illustrations of *les gosses de Paris* (the children of Paris), are still reproduced today. Many of the drawings in this sketchbook are either excellent copies of his work or originals.

G. Douanne
(French, dates unknown)
"I Am a Fine War Hen. I Eat Little and
I Produce a Lot," 1918
LITHOGRAPH

This poster by a 16-year-old French schoolgirl was
a winning design in a contest held by the Minister
of Education. In contrast to most French poster art
during the war, this drawing is rich with color and
delightful naïveté.

>>>

Joseph Parphyre Pinchon's *Bécassine chez les alliés*
(Paris: H. Gautier, 1917)

Pinchon (1871–1953) created the character Bécassine, an intrepid housemaid from Brittany, France, who is
considered the first female comic-book protagonist. Although always drawn wearing her traditional Breton
costume and portrayed as a simple, naïve country girl, she manages to outwit her craftier nemeses. In this
work, Bécassine helps a Scottish pilot take aerial photographs, attends a war conference with Maréchal Joffre,
and captures a German spy.

Unidentified artist
"A Million Boys Behind a Million Fighters—Every American Boy Should Enroll in the Victory Boys," 1918
LITHOGRAPH

In 1918 the United War Work Campaign introduced youth organizations called "Victory Boys" and "Victory Girls." These groups encouraged schoolchildren to dedicate their time, labor, and earnings to the war effort. Unlike the Boy Scouts of America, Victory Boys and Girls did not publicly solicit money. Instead, they were encouraged to work after-school jobs so that they themselves could "earn and give" to the United War Work Campaign fund. The families of participating children were encouraged to hang "Victory" banners in the windows of their homes.

<<< FACING PAGE, TOP RIGHT

Maginel Wright Enright
(American, 1881–1966)
"Follow the Pied Piper—Join the United States School Garden Army," 1918
LITHOGRAPH

In 1917 the U.S. Bureau of Education, with funding from the War Department, spearheaded the United States Garden Army, an effort to encourage schoolchildren and their teachers to grow extra food to feed troops abroad. The Bureau of Education distributed books and manuals that taught urban and suburban children how to tend soil, raise fruits and vegetables, and can food. Children learned about landscaping, botany, and nutrition while helping curtail the drastic food shortage brought on by the war. The image of Uncle Sam as the Pied Piper appeared on the majority of manuals distributed to schools across the nation. The image was designed by children's book illustrator Maginel Wright Enright, sister of architect Frank Lloyd Wright. The United States Garden Army's official slogan was "A garden for every child, every child in a garden."

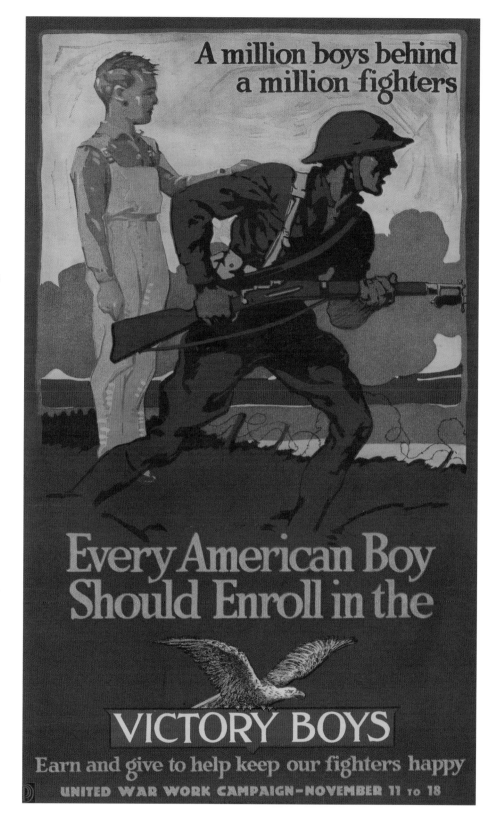

Edward Penfield
(American, 1866–1925)
"Every Girl Pulling for Victory—Victory Girls," 1918
LITHOGRAPH

The Lost

Wilfred Owen's last letter to his mother, Susan Owen
October 31, 1918

Owen composed this last letter to his mother in the smoky cellar of a French farmhouse, just a few days before being killed by machine-gun fire on the Sambre-Oise Canal. Reflecting on the camaraderie of the men, he writes: "It is a great life. I am more oblivious than alas! yourself, dear Mother, of the ghastly glimmering of the guns outside, & the hollow crashing of the shells. . . . Of this I am certain you could not be visited by a band of friends half so fine as surround me here."

Owen was killed one week before the universal stand-down to arms. In 2011 the farmhouse in which Owen wrote this letter was turned into a memorial for the fallen soldiers of the Western Front.

Letter from Edward Thomas
to Edward Garnett
January 13, 1917

In this letter written from a British army base, poet Edward Thomas says good-bye to one of his oldest and best friends, writer and editor Edward Garnett. The two men met long before the war and for years were leading members of the "Mont Blanc" literary club, named for the French restaurant in Soho where they met. A friend, mentor, neighbor, and fishing partner, Garnett was a tremendous influence on the younger Thomas, who dedicated *The South Country* to Garnett in 1909.

   Upon the outbreak of war, Garnett used his influence to try to secure a home-service posting for Thomas but was not successful. Thomas was killed by an exploding shell during the first hours of the Battle of Arras on April 9, 1917. Another close friend of Thomas's, American poet Robert Frost, wrote of Thomas that "his last word to me, his 'pen ultimate word' as he called it, was that what he cared most for was the name of poet."

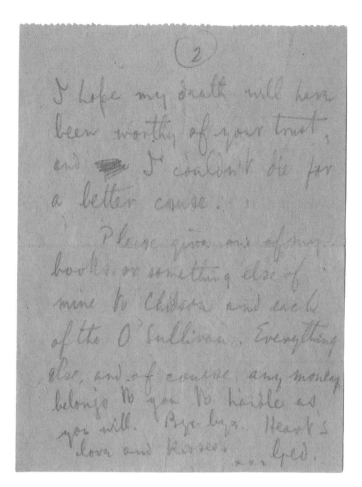

‹‹‹

Roland Garvin's last letter to his parents
July 20, 1916

Roland Garvin, known as "Ged," was the son of newspaper editor J. L. Garvin. In what became his last letter to his parents, he writes from a ravine near Memetz Wood: "This is just a short note for you. We go into action in a day or two and I'm leaving this in case I don't come back. It brings you both, and to the girls and Granny, my very deepest love. Try not to grieve too much for me. . . . I hope my death will have been worthy of your trust and I couldn't die for a better cause. . . . Heart's love and kisses. xxx Ged."

Garvin wrote a letter to his son on July 21, but that letter and others sent before Garvin learned of his son's death were returned to Garvin stamped "Return to Sender" and "Killed in Action." Ged likely died shortly after midnight on July 23, killed by machine-gun fire while leading his company in a night assault on a strongly fortified German line north of Bazentin-le-Petit. His body was never recovered.

Third sitting Nov. 1918.

Kingsley is here. Apologises for barging in.

His mother is in the spirit world with him.
Calls me Dad.
Can help me now more than before.
He wouldn't in any case has stayed in Old England
Wisdom is behind his death
Plenty to take care of him over there.
Malcolm is with him - they talk much of
medical things, want to set the world on fire
with medical knowledge.
Says I saw him once since he passed.
He didn't stand an earthly in his illness
Pain in his lungs
Tried hard not to die.
Wanted to send his love to Jean & the little ones.

    Also to Elizabeth, Vera, Nora, Mayory.
He is a new scholar but learning well
AMY is helping him. You will know her by
violets.
ALEC there
Also Dick or Richard & Uncle Henry.
Mother had died from throat.
He is now in sympathy with Spiritualism.
Thought before that I was being bamboozled
Give little JOHN his love - would like to
squeeze him. Also little JEAN.

My son had died 6 weeks
before. His name was
given as Arthur in the
papers.

    Yes.

That is good - usually
      DADSY.

    true

That is true but I had
foolishly told the medium

All wrong, so far as I know.

Very good. AMY HOARE.
Violets her favourite flower

names right

Right

Both very good.

‹‹‹

Arthur Conan Doyle's record of a sitting with a spirit medium
November 1918

Sir Arthur Conan Doyle (1859–1930) began writing and lecturing about his belief in Spiritualism during the war "when all these splendid fellows were disappearing from our view." His son, Arthur Alleyne Kingsley Doyle, known as Kingsley, died in October 1918 of pneumonia contracted while recuperating from serious injuries sustained at the Battle of the Somme in 1916.

In this record of a personal sitting in which the spirit of Kingsley visits, Doyle records the medium's message in the left-hand column and his own assessment of its validity in the right-hand column.

MEDIUM	DOYLE
Kingsley is here. Apologises for barging in.	My son had died 6 weeks before. His name was given as Arthur in the papers.
Calls me Dad.	That is good. Usually Dadsy.

New York Journal-American
Mother and coffin, Hoboken, New Jersey,
not dated
GELATIN SILVER PRINT

The mother of an American soldier lifts the flag draped over the coffin of her son, a private in the American Expeditionary Force. Though General Pershing favored burying fallen American soldiers near the battlefields where they died, surviving relatives of the soldiers were given the choice of having their loved ones permanently interred in large overseas cemeteries or brought back to the United States for reburial. When the war ended, the families of 43,909 dead troops asked for their remains to be brought back to the United States by boat, while roughly 20,000 chose to have the bodies remain in Europe. The first bodies of troops killed in the conflict were not sent back to the United States until 1921.

<<<

Postcard photograph of Isaac Rosenberg

not dated

≋

Manuscript of Rosenberg's "The Dying Soldier"

not dated

Poet and painter Isaac Rosenberg (1890–1918) is considered one of the greatest English war poets. Critical of the war from the outset, Rosenberg never-theless enlisted to help support his mother and was killed in France on April 1, 1918. "Killed in Action," Rosenberg's remarkable eulogy to himself, "so poor an outward man," references his chronic poor health and his stature. He was initially assigned to a "ban-tam" battalion of men who stood less than five feet three inches tall.

>>> FACING PAGE

Frank Lucien Nicolet

(Canadian, 1887–?)

"If ye break faith / We shall not sleep," 1918

LITHOGRAPH

John McCrae's "In Flanders Fields" is one of the best-remembered and most-often-quoted poems of the First World War and established the red poppy as the emblem of those lost during the conflict.

McCrae (1872–1918), a Canadian doctor and soldier, wrote the poem after the death of a friend and former student in the first attack of the Ypres Salient in 1915. McCrae's poem describes the blood-red poppies that proliferated on the battlefields and cemeteries in Flanders. The specific species of poppy that McCrae indicates (*Papaver rhoes*) thrives in upturned soil, which the trenches and shell holes of the Western Front supplied in abundance.

This poster, which features a Canadian soldier mourning the dead in a field of scarlet flowers, invokes McCrae's poem to warn the civilian not to forget the sacrifices made by soldiers. The quotation is from the last stanza of "In Flanders Fields":

> In Flanders fields the poppies blow
> Between the crosses, row on row,
> That mark our place; and in the sky
> The larks, still bravely singing, fly
> Scarce heard amid the guns below.
>
> We are the Dead. Short days ago
> We lived, felt dawn, saw sunset glow,
> Loved and were loved, and now we lie
> In Flanders fields.
>
> Take up our quarrel with the foe:
> To you from failing hands we throw
> The torch; be yours to hold it high.
> If ye break faith with us who die
> We shall not sleep, though poppies grow
> In Flanders fields.

INDEX